Ottawa Ontario Book 2 in Colour Photos, Saving Our History One Photo at a Time

Photography
by Barbara Raué
2016

Series Name:
Cruising Ontario

Book 147: Ottawa Book 2

Cover photo: 555 Mackenzie Avenue, Page 33

Series Name: Cruising Ontario
Saving Our History One Photo at a Time
in colour photos

Books Available in Alphabetical Order:
Aberfoyle, Acton, Alton, Amherstburg, Ancaster, Arthur, Aylmer, Ayr, Bloomingdale, Brantford, Burlington, Caledon, Caledonia, Cambridge, Clifford, Conestogo, Delhi, Dorchester to Aylmer, Drayton, Drumbo, Dundas, Eden Mills, Elmira, Elora, Essex, Fergus, Guelph, Hagersville, Hamilton, Hanover, Harriston, Hespeler, Jarvis, Kingston, Kingsville, Kitchener, Linwood, Listowel, London, Lucknow, Mono, Mount Forest, Neustadt, New Hamburg, Niagara-on-the-Lake, Oakville, Orangeville, Orillia, Owen Sound, Palmerston, Peterborough, Petrolia, Port Elgin, Preston, Rockwood, Sarnia, Seaforth, Sheffield, Shelburne, Simcoe, Southampton, St. Jacobs, St. Marys, St. Thomas, Stoney Creek, Stratford, Thamesford, Tillsonburg, Waterdown, Waterford, Waterloo, Welland, Wellesley, Windsor, Wingham, Woodstock

Book 123-124: Kingsville
Book 125-127: Woodstock
Book 128: Thamesford
Book 129-132: St. Marys
Book 133-136: Sarnia
Book 137: Petrolia
Book 138-139: Welland
Book 140-145: Kingston
Book 146-149: Ottawa

Other Books by Barbara Raue

Coins of Gold

Arrows, Indians and Love

The Life and Times of Barbara
Volume 1: Inventions That Have Enhanced My Life
Volume 2: Entertainment That I Have Enjoyed
Volume 3: East Coast Trips
Volume 4: Olympics Have Always Intrigued Me
Volume 5: Wonders of the World
Volume 6: Caribbean Cruises We Have Enjoyed
Volume 7: Animals
Volume 8: Storms and Other Major Disasters in My Lifetime
Volume 9: Wars, Terrorist Attacks and Major Disasters

The Cromwell Family Book

Laura Secord Discovered

Daddy Where Are You?

Montana Series
Book 1: Montana Dream
Book 2: Life on the Montana Frontier
Book 3: Montana to Boston and Back

Visit Barbara's website to view all of her books
http://barbararaue.ca

Table of Contents

Canada became a nation, the Dominion of Canada, in 1867. Before that, British North America was made up of a few provinces, the vast area of Rupert's Land (privately owned by the Hudson's Bay Company), and the North-Western Territory. By 1864, many leaders felt it would be good to join into one country. These leaders met and wrote a constitution for the new country, which had to be passed by the Parliament of the United Kingdom. Once passed, it became known as the *British North America Act* which brought together the three provinces of Nova Scotia, New Brunswick and Canada (which became the provinces of Ontario and Quebec). Manitoba and the Northwest Territories joined in 1870, British Columbia in 1871, Prince Edward Island in 1873, Yukon Territory in 1898, Alberta and Saskatchewan in 1905, Newfoundland and Labrador not until 1949, and Nunavut separated from the Northwest Territories as its own unit in 1999.

In the 1890s, when Prime Minister Sir Wilfrid Laurier spoke of making Ottawa a "Washington of the North", he wanted a new architectural style for the Capital that was distinct from American and older British models, in pursuit of grandeur.

In 1982, the Queen and the Right Honourable Pierre Trudeau, Prime Minister, signed the *Constitution Act, 1982* to make Canada an independent nation.

The Heritage Building is today part of Ottawa City Hall. It was originally built in 1874 as Ottawa Normal School and served as a teacher's college. The Gothic Revival building stands at Elgin and Lisgar Streets; several extensions were added to the rear of the building. In the 1960s the Ontario's teachers' colleges were merged into universities and this one was merged into the Faculty of Education of the University of Ottawa in 1974.

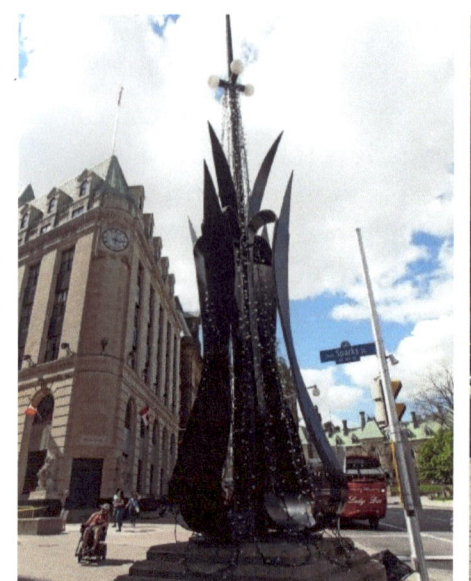 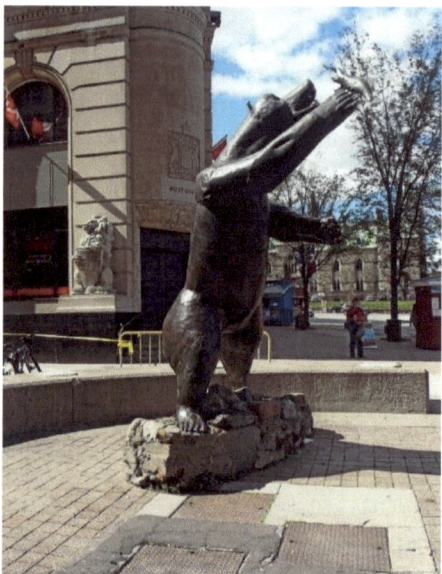

Sparks Street

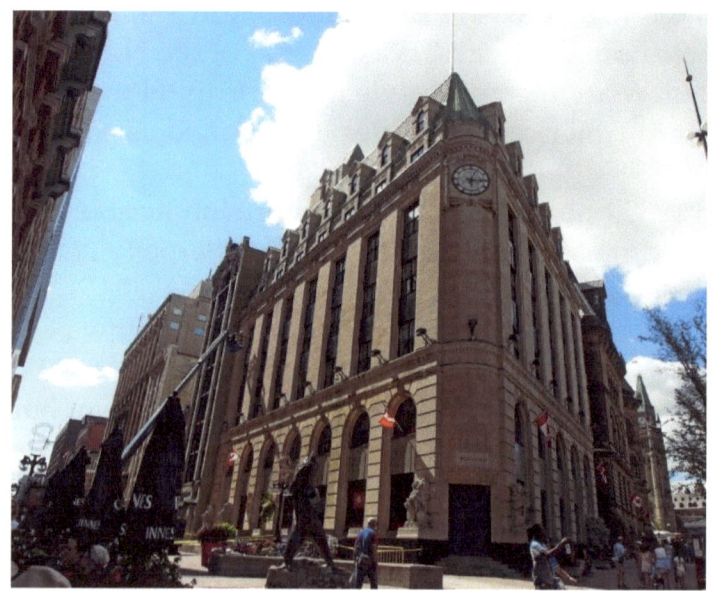

59 Sparks Street – 1939 - Post Office – Chateauesque and
Art Deco styles

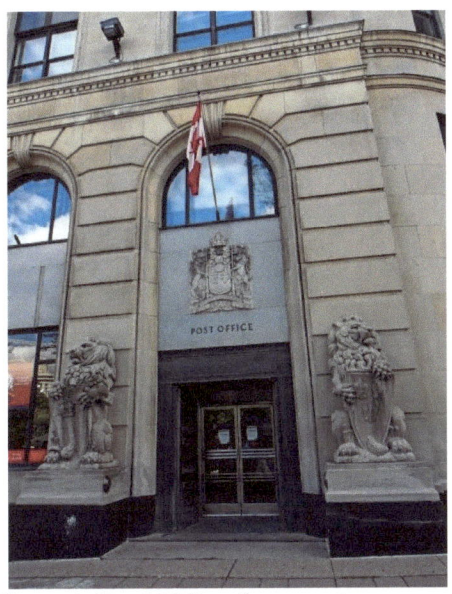

Post Office, A.D. 1939 - decorative carved lions

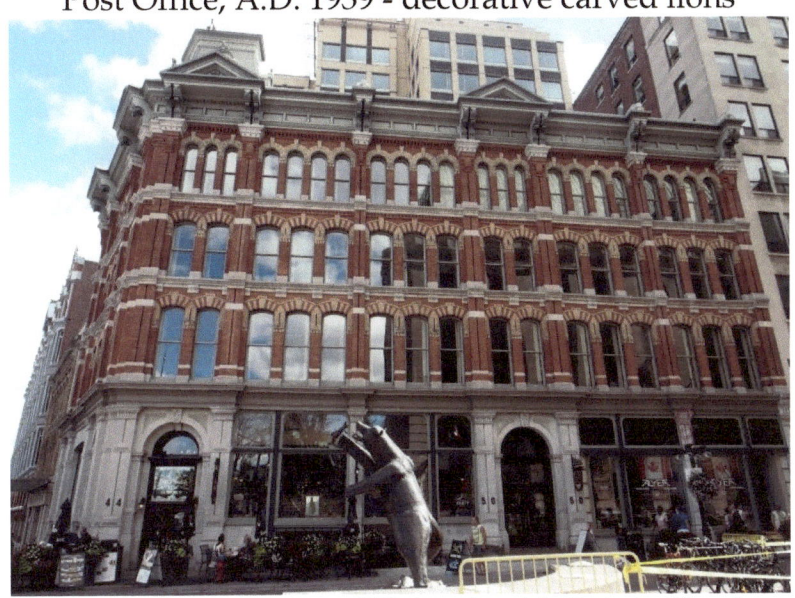

44-50 Sparks Street at corner of Elgin – Scottish Ontario Chambers –
Italianate design - four-storey brick building with a high ground floor,
balanced façade, decorative multi-coloured masonry, radiated voussoirs of
multicolored brick, fenestration (the arrangement, design and
proportioning of windows and doors), roof line with heavy bracketing and
decorated cornice

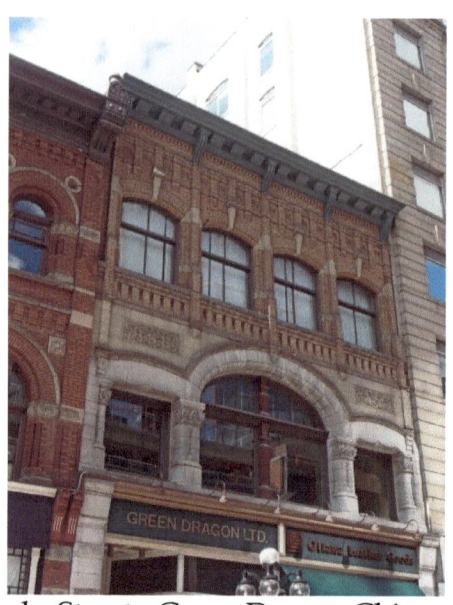

167 Sparks Street - Green Dragon Chinese Gifts, Ottawa Leather Goods – cornice brackets, dentil moulding, voussoirs and keystones, columns with Corinthian capitals with central arch

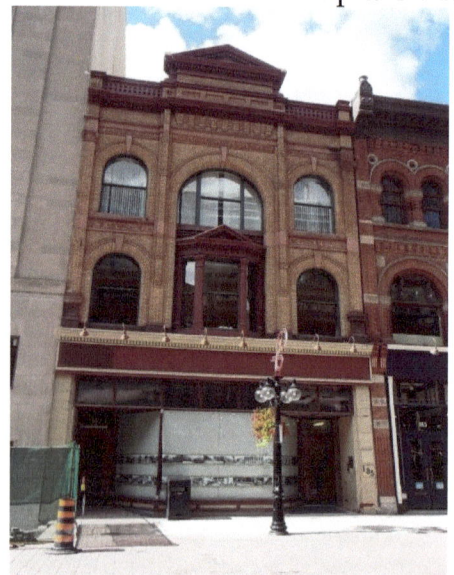

185-187 Sparks Street – pilasters, decorative banding, voussoirs with keystones, bay window with pediment and decorative cornice, dentil moulding, raised centre section with pediment

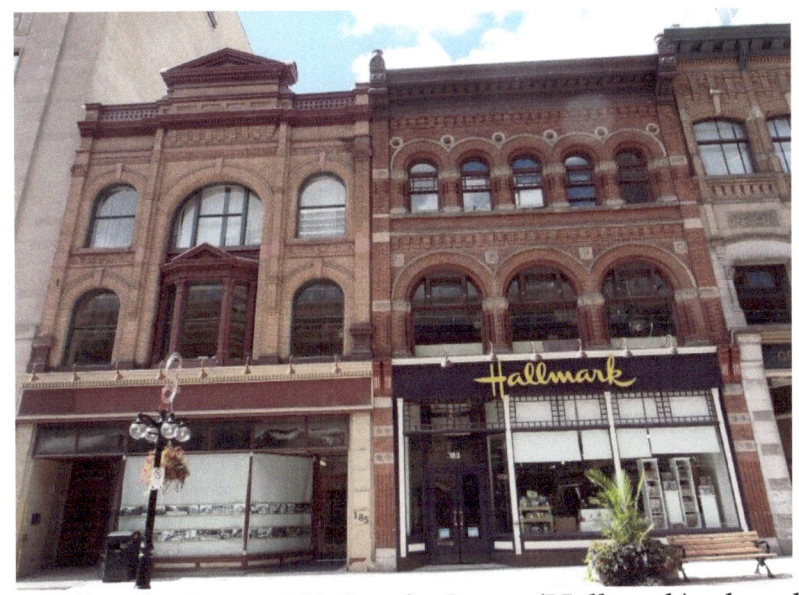

185-187 Sparks Street; 183 Sparks Street (Hallmark) – bevelled
dentil moulding

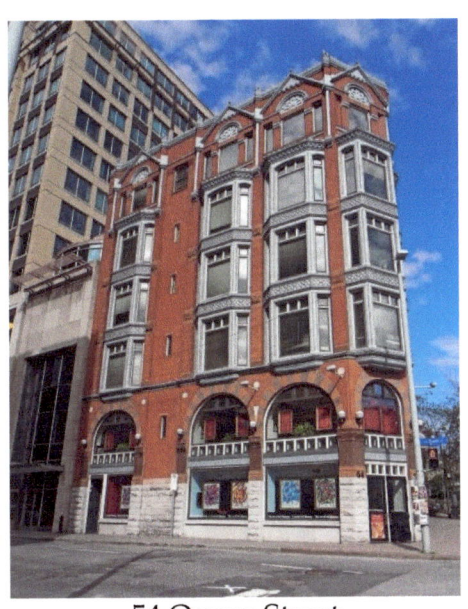

54 Queen Street

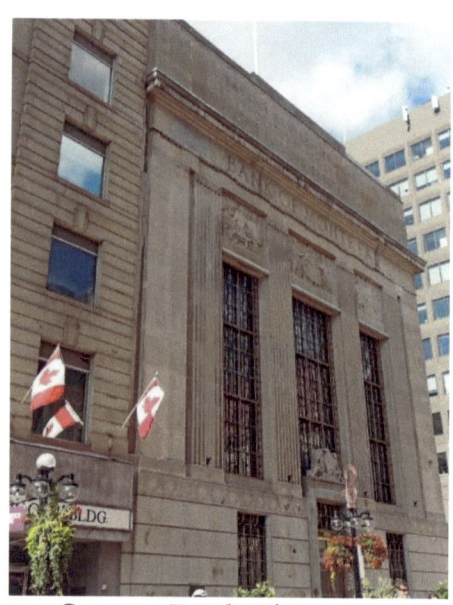

144 Wellington Street - Bank of Montreal founded 1817
- Art Deco design

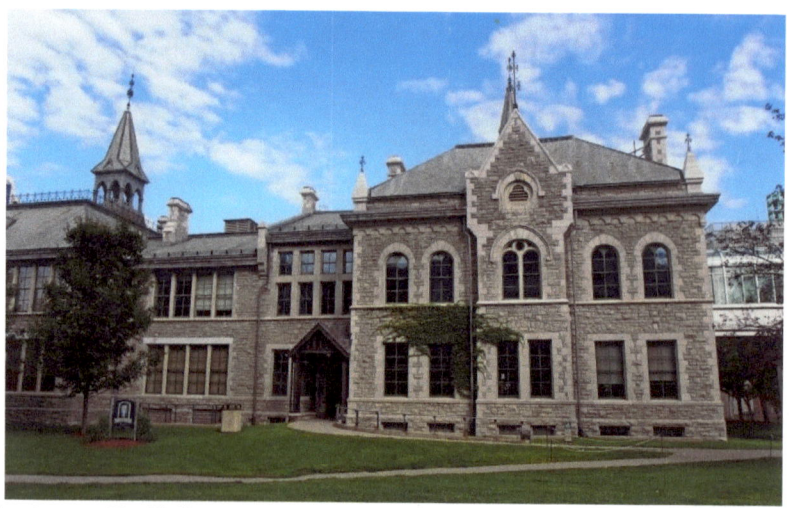

Heritage Building section of Ottawa City Hall facing Elgin
Street (old Ottawa Normal School) – 1874 – Jacobean gable on
frontispiece with trefoil in gable, decorative cornice scalloping

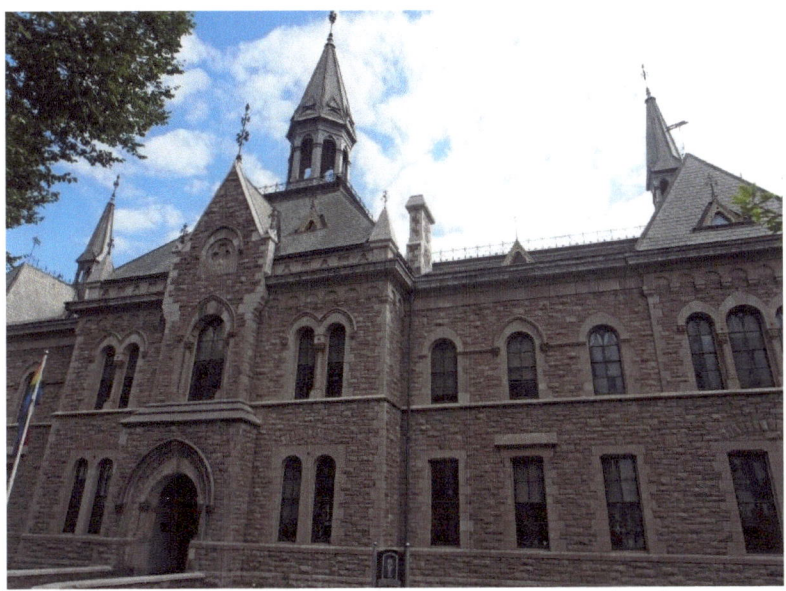

Cupola, stone and brick construction materials, drip moulds ending in human heads and other designs, columns with Corinthian capitals between paired windows

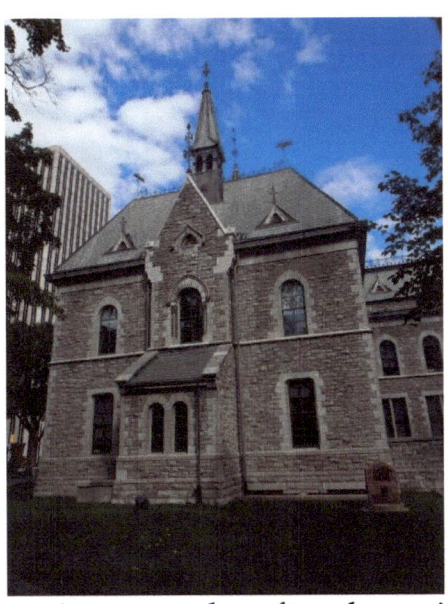

Iron cresting around rooftop, bay window

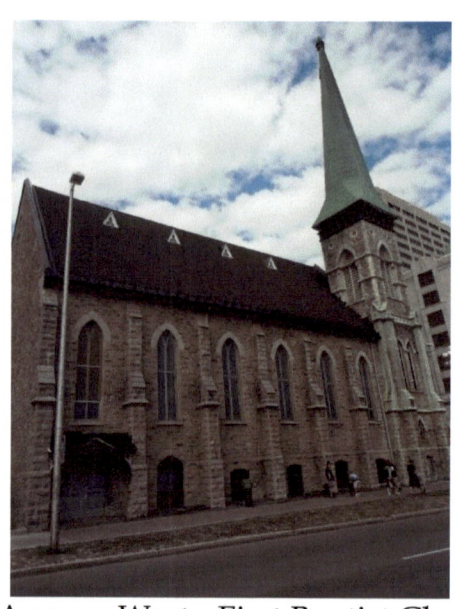

140 Laurier Avenue West - First Baptist Church – Gothic Revival – buttresses, rose window, lancet windows, copper-covered spire

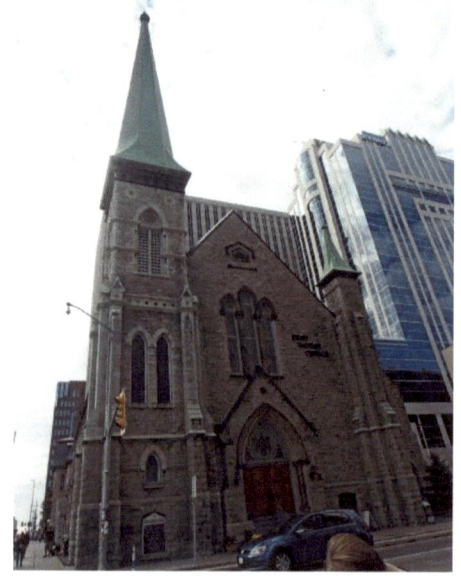

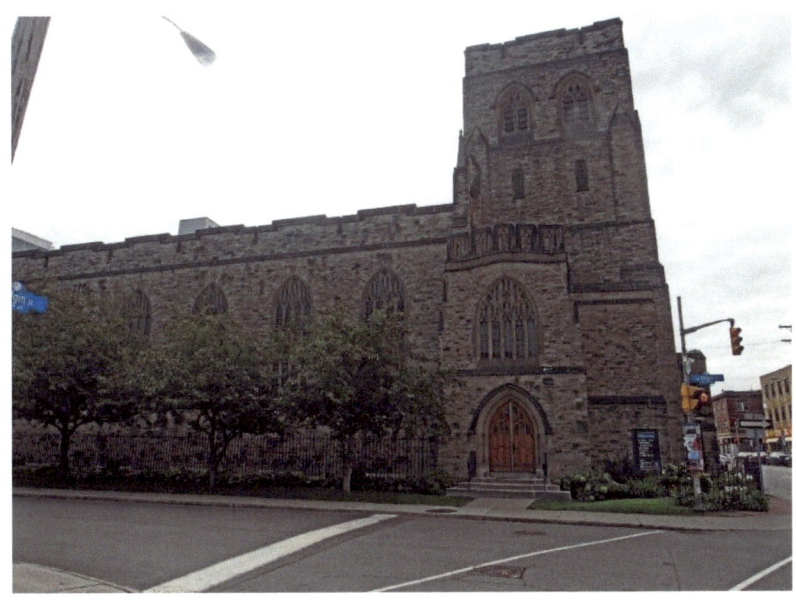

120 Lisgar Street – Knox Presbyterian Church – Gothic Revival
– wimpergs, crenellation, quatrefoil, muntins and mullions

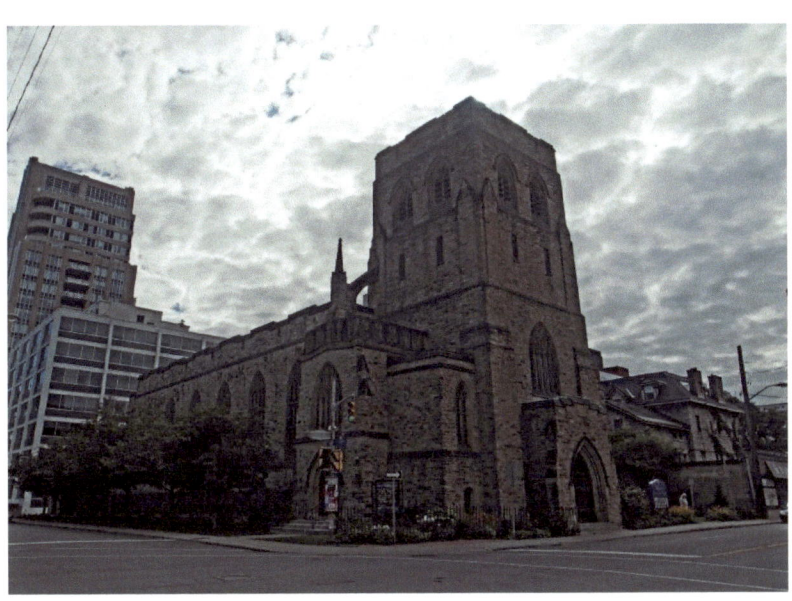

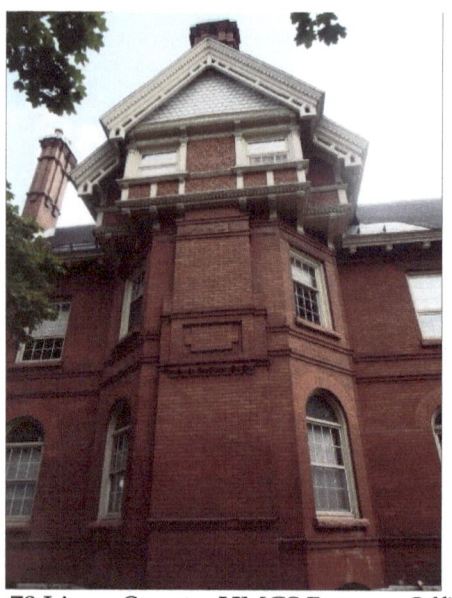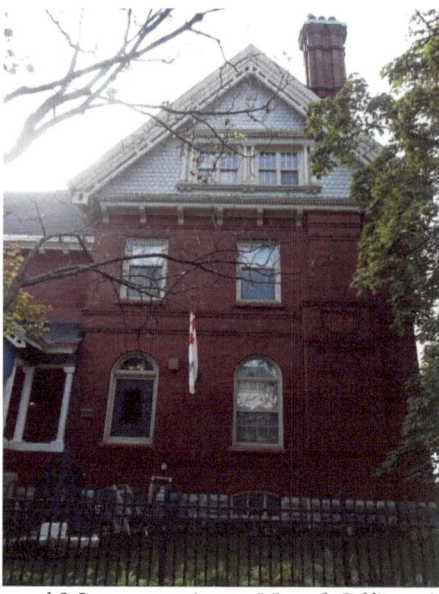

78 Lisgar Street – HMCS Bytown Officers' Mess - a private Naval Officers' Mess – house built in 1896 – banding, cornice brackets, verge board trim on gable

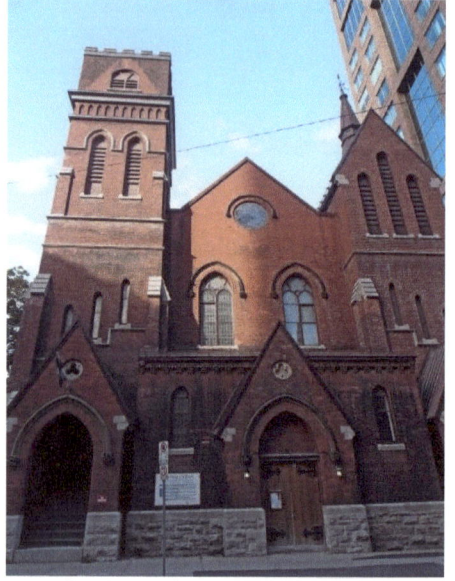

152 Metcalfe Street - St. Peter & St. Paul's Anglican Church (formerly known as St. George's) - built as a Methodist Episcopal church at the corner of Metcalfe and Gloucester – Gothic Revival - trefoils in lower gables, crenellated tower, rose window, dentil molding

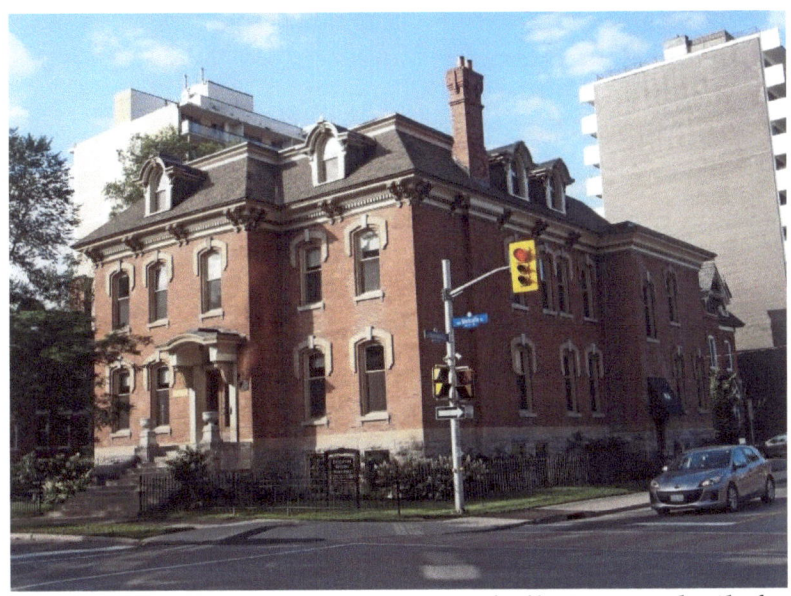

236 Metcalfe Street – 1883 – Campbell House – built for
Senator Alexander Campbell, a Father of Confederation
Second Empire style – dormers with window hoods,
keystones, paired cornice brackets

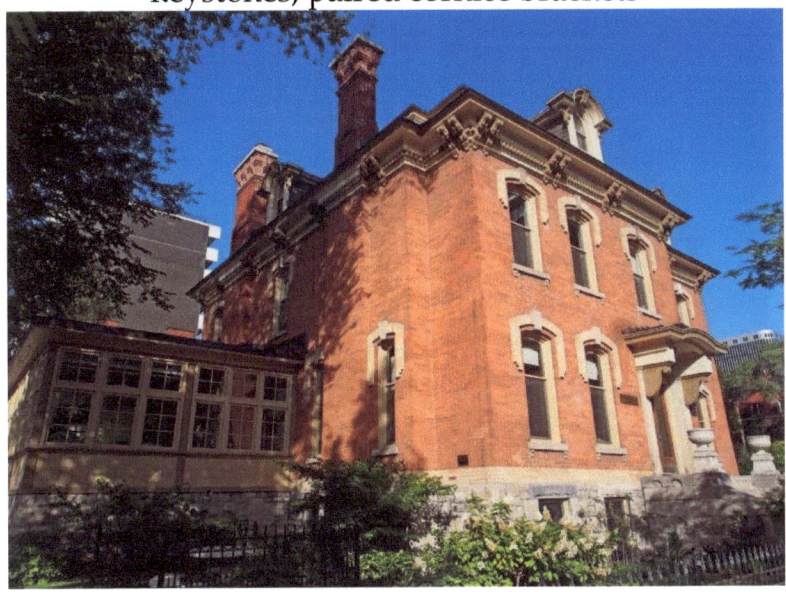

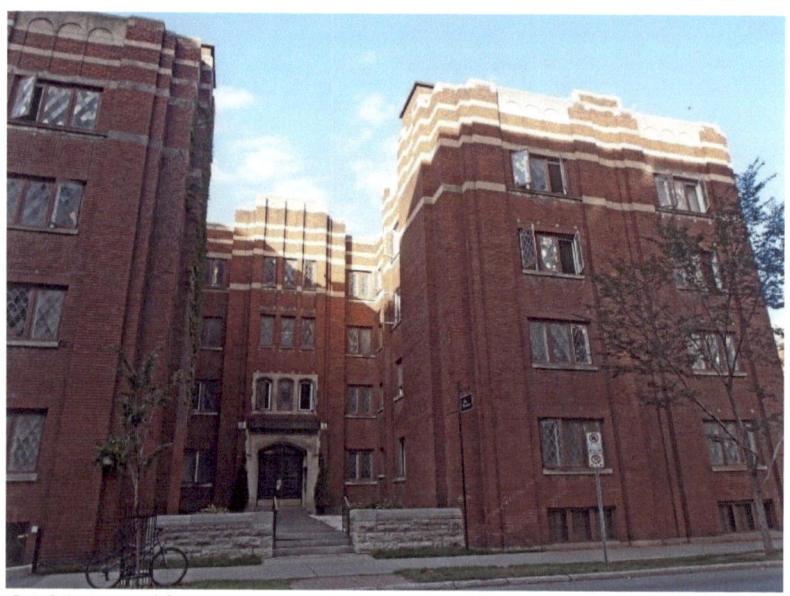

216 Metcalfe Street - The Duncannon – 1931 - banding

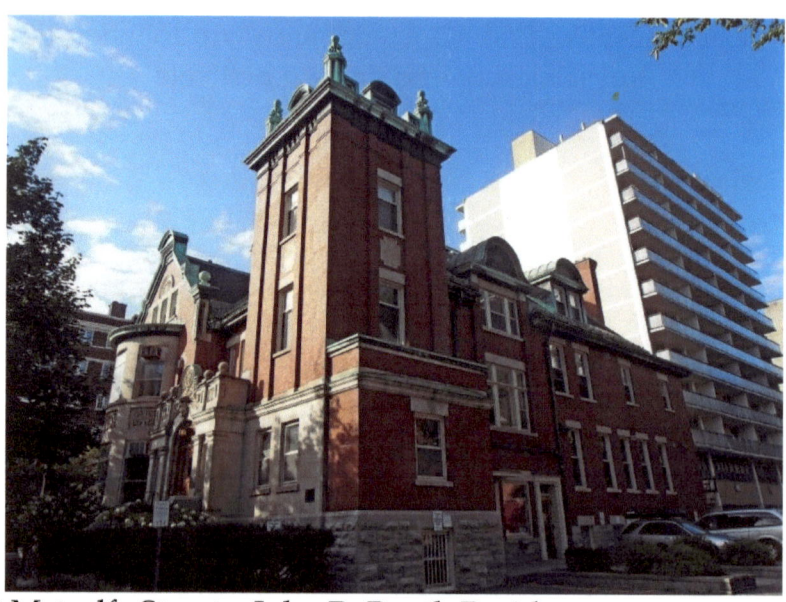

252 Metcalfe Street – John R. Booth Residence – square corner tower surmounted by finely sculpted finials to create a house of baronial grandeur

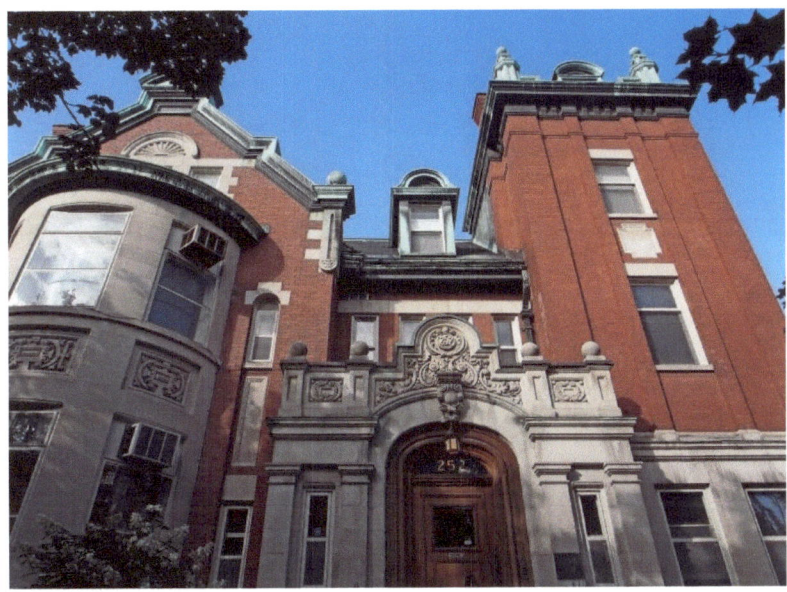

252 Metcalfe Street – Queen Anne Revival – built by lumber baron John R. Booth 1906-1909 – elaborately shaped gables, ornate stone moulding, intersecting ridges of the roof

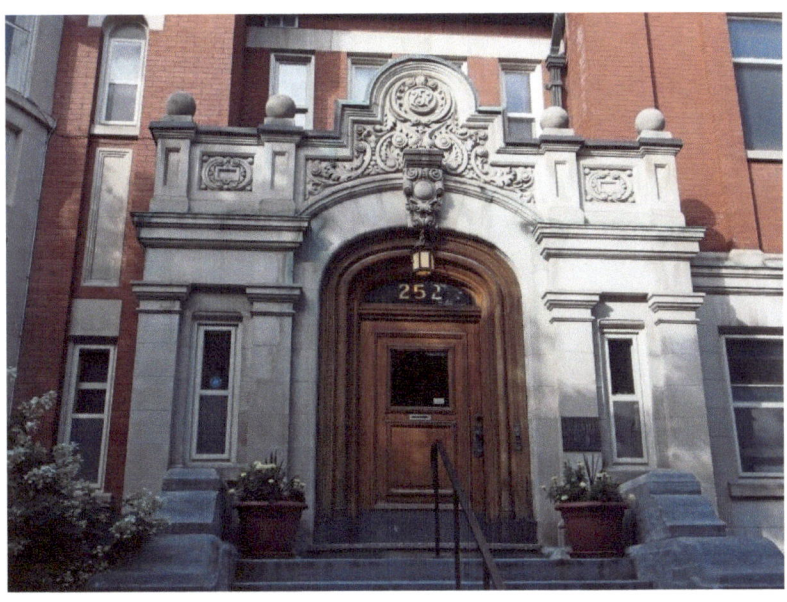

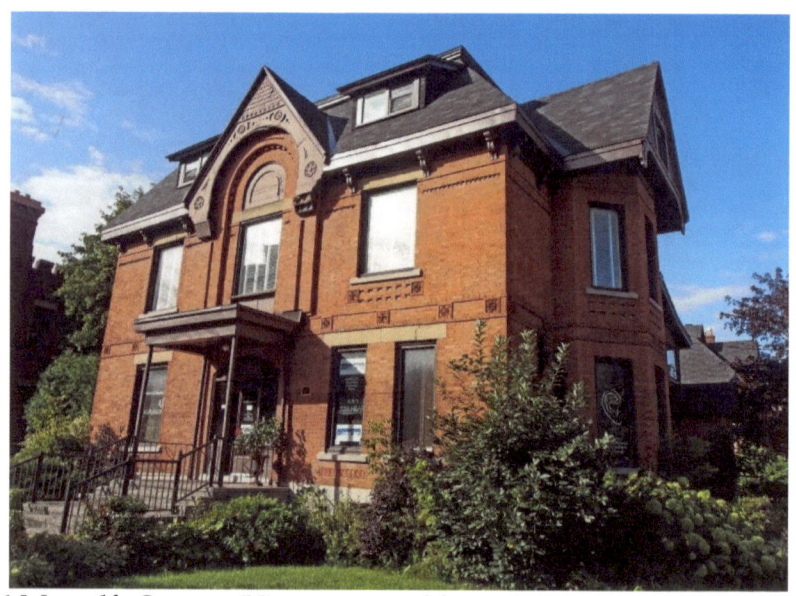

296 Metcalfe Street – Victorian - gable with verge board trim, roof dormer, terra cotta decoration

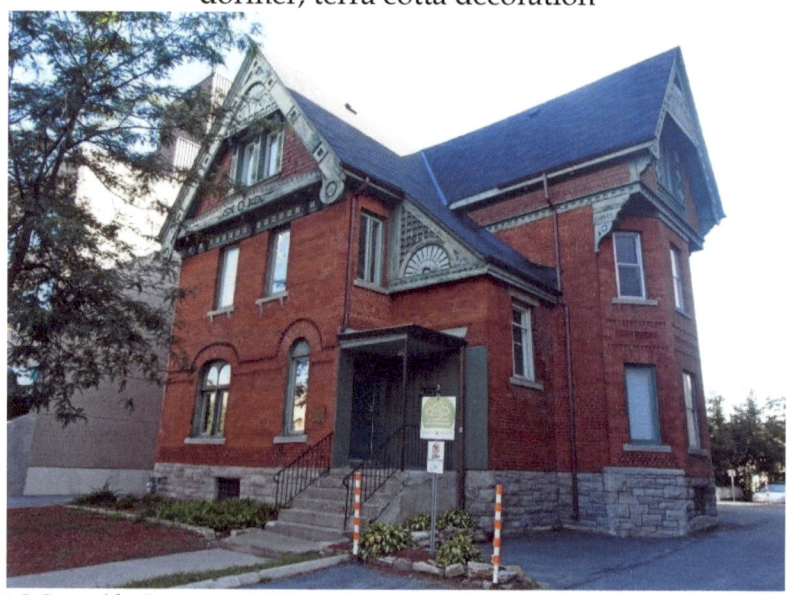

301 Metcalfe Street – 1889 – designed by Frederick J. Alexander – Queen Anne style – was the home of Douglas Brymner, first Dominion archivist, and father of prominent painter William Brymner – verge board trim, fretwork

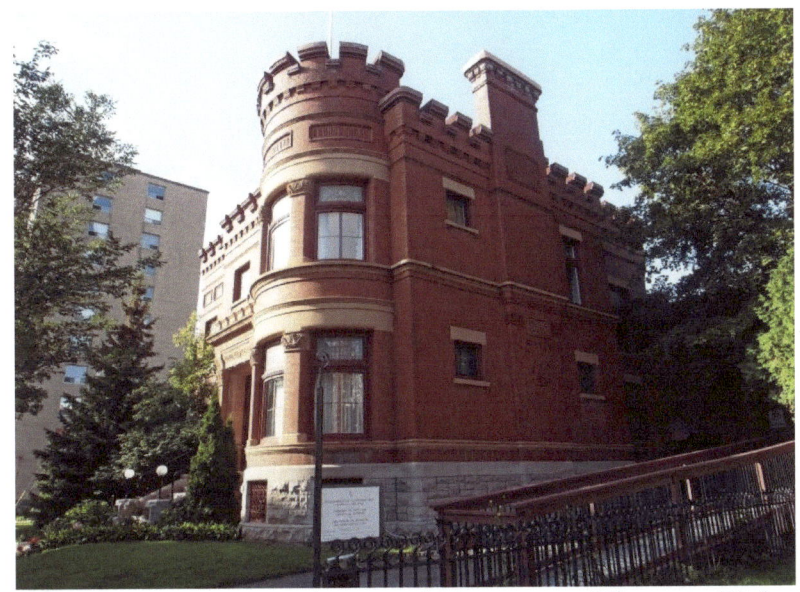

306 Metcalfe Street - Embassy of Hungary - Thomas Birkett, a hardware merchant, an alderman, Mayor of Ottawa, and MP at the turn of the 20th Century, built Birkett Castle in 1896. It is a rare example of Baronial Gothic architecture with towers, a crenellated roofline, and columns with composite capitals.

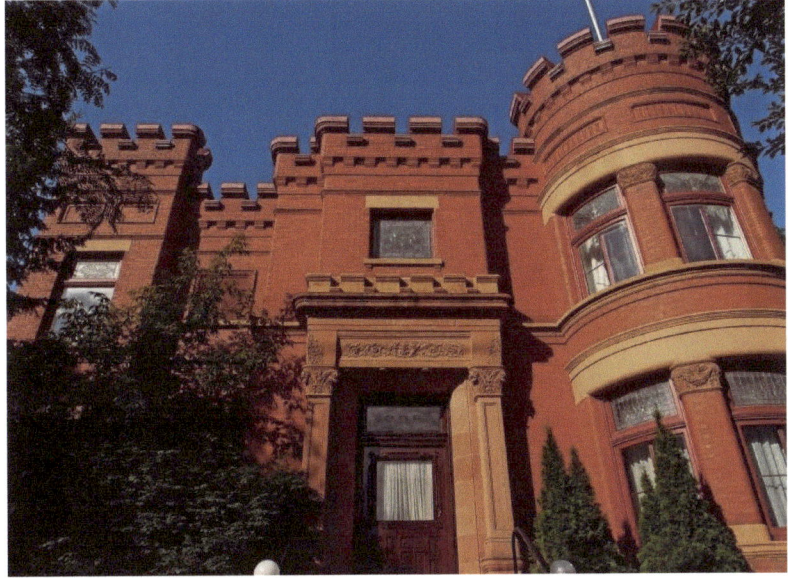

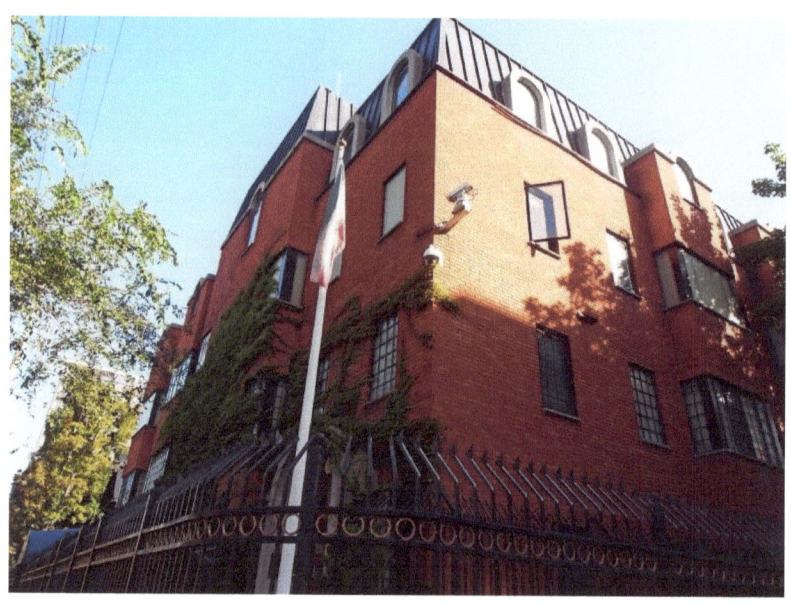

245 Metcalfe Street – Embassy of the Islamic Republic of Iran

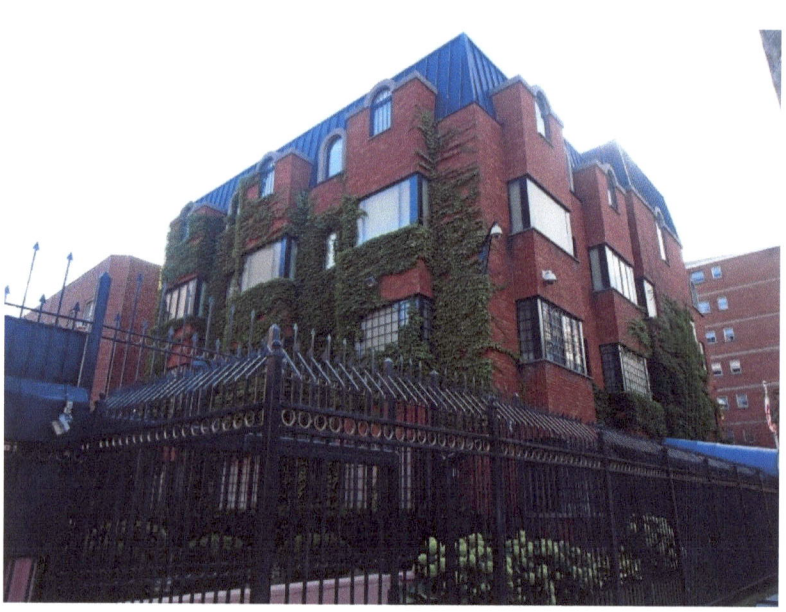

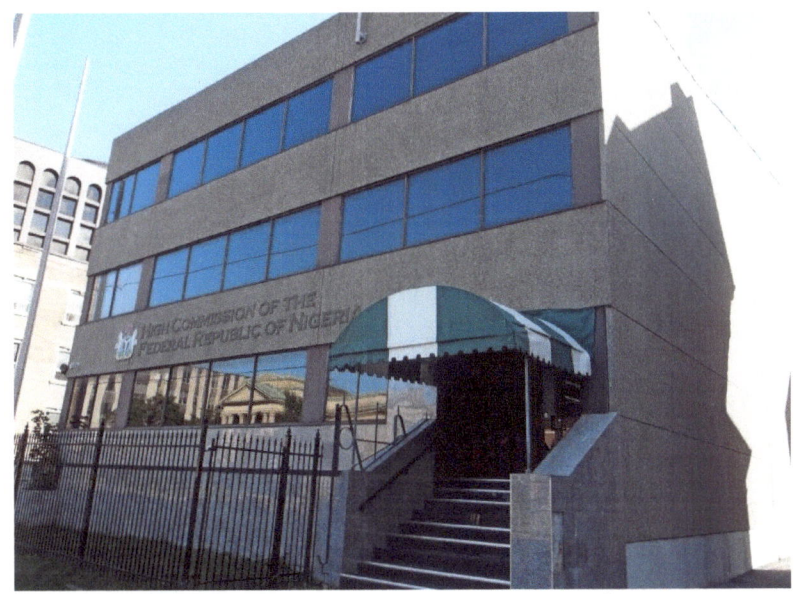

295 Metcalfe Street - Nigerian Embassy

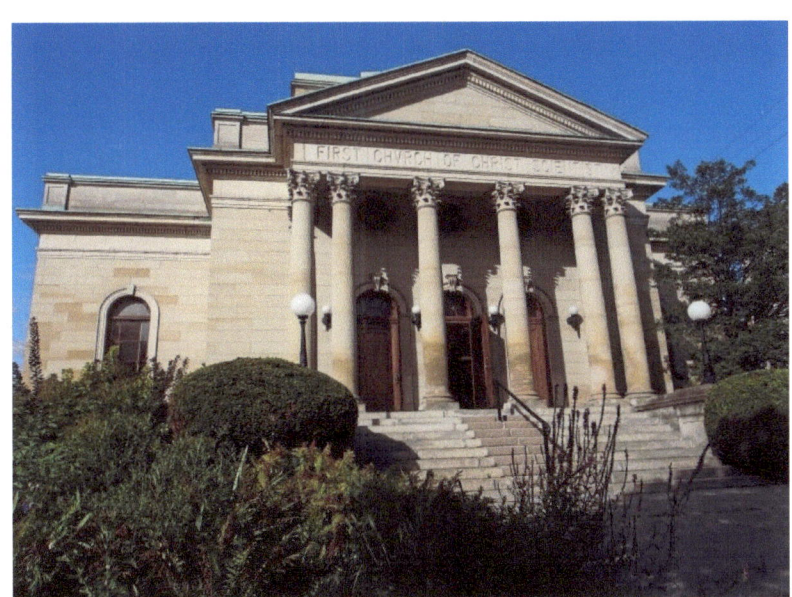

280 Gilmour Street - First Church of Christ Scientist – 1913 –
Italianate style - six columns with composite capitals
supporting a pediment

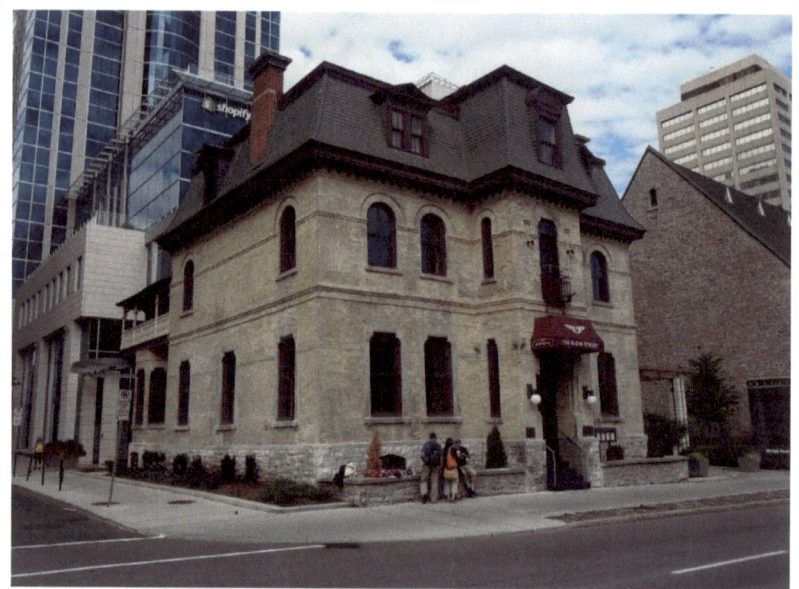

150 Elgin Street - 1875 - Grant House – Second Empire style – 2½ storey brick built for Sir James Grant, M.P., a prominent physician

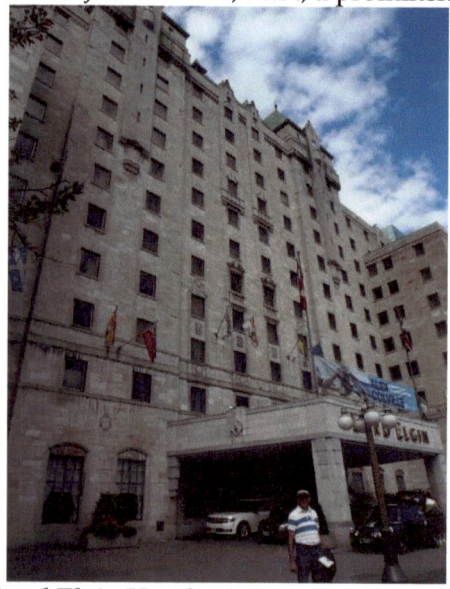

100 Elgin Street - Lord Elgin Hotel – A.D. 1941 – named after James Bruce, 8th Earl of Elgin, first Governor General of united Canadas - 12 storeys – limestone walls with broken courses, flattened oriel windows and modernistic chevrons - topped by a steep copper chateauesque roof

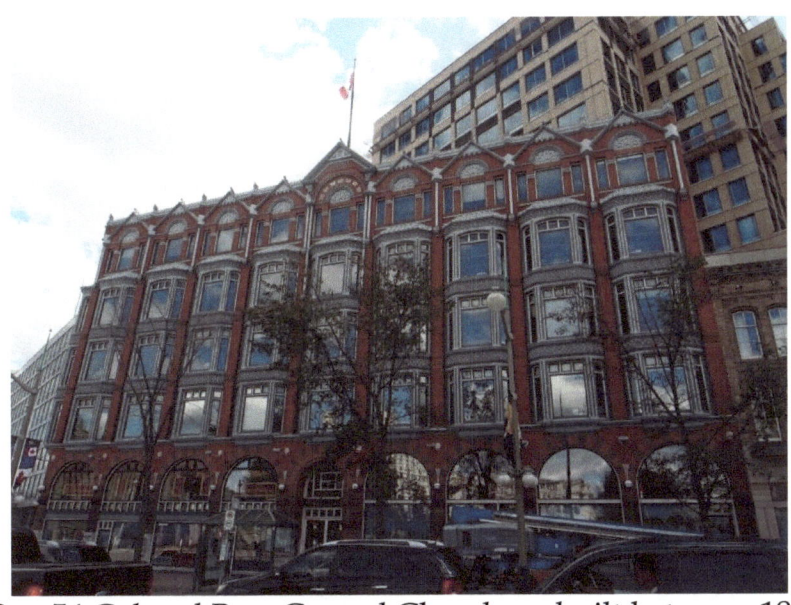

42 to 54 Colonel By – Central Chamber - built between 1890 and 1893 – Queen Anne Revival commercial architecture

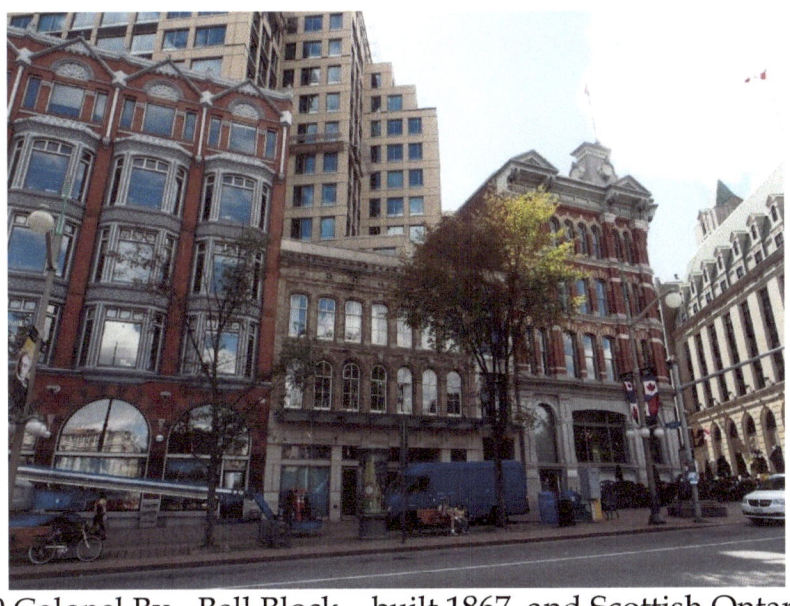

40 Colonel By - Bell Block – built 1867, and Scottish Ontario Chambers (Canadian Pacific Railways building) on corner of Sparks and Elgin Streets

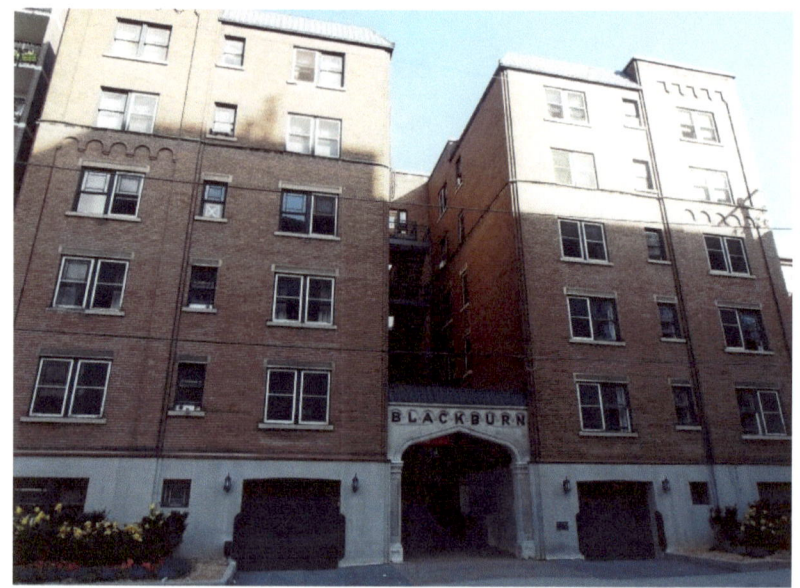

223 Somerset Avenue West – Blackburn apartments

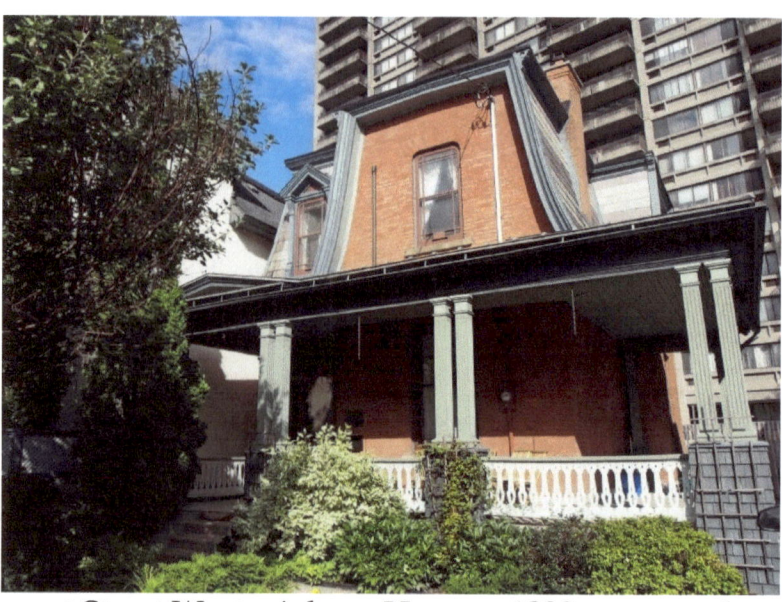

Somerset Street West - Adams House – 1888 – vernacular style

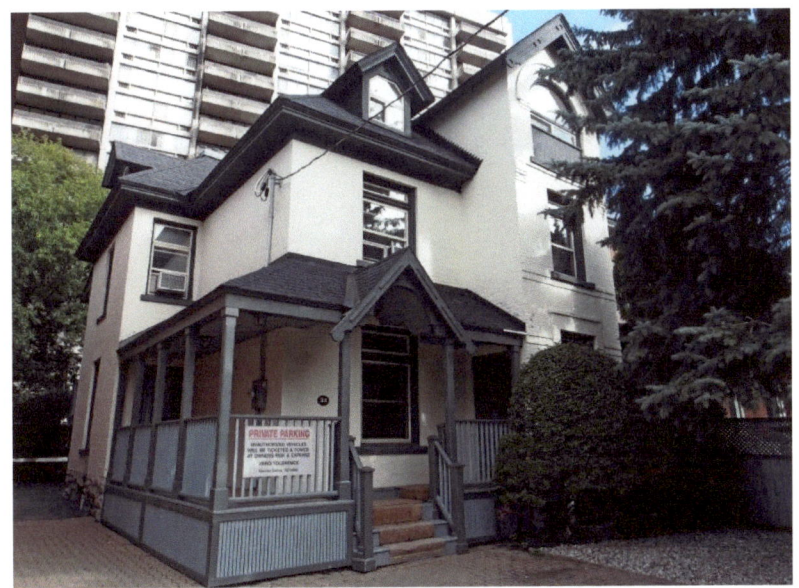

33 Somerset Street West

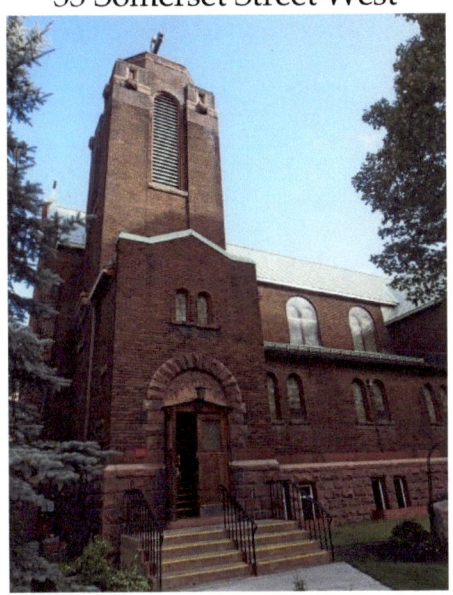

95 Somerset Street West at corner of Cartier Street - St. Theresa's Roman Catholic Church – 1933 – Romanesque Revival

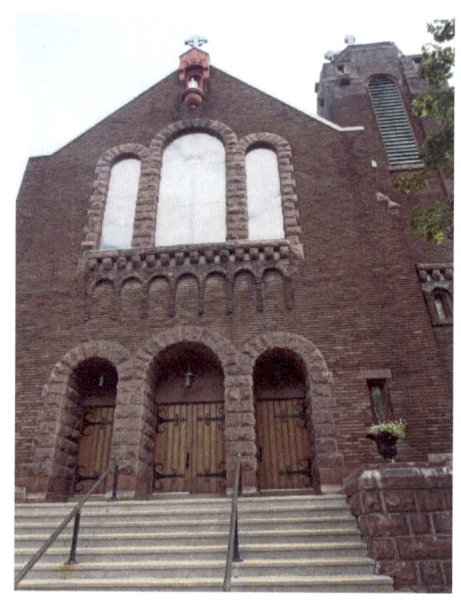

95 Somerset Street

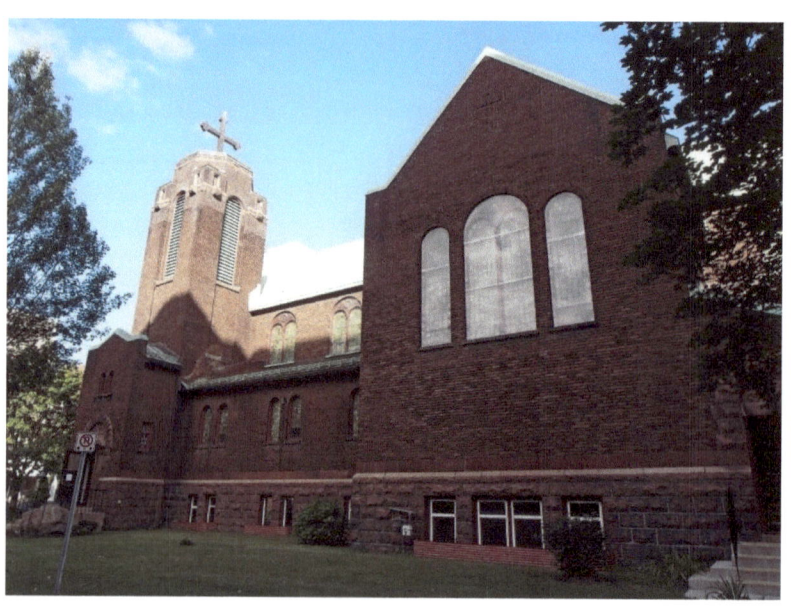

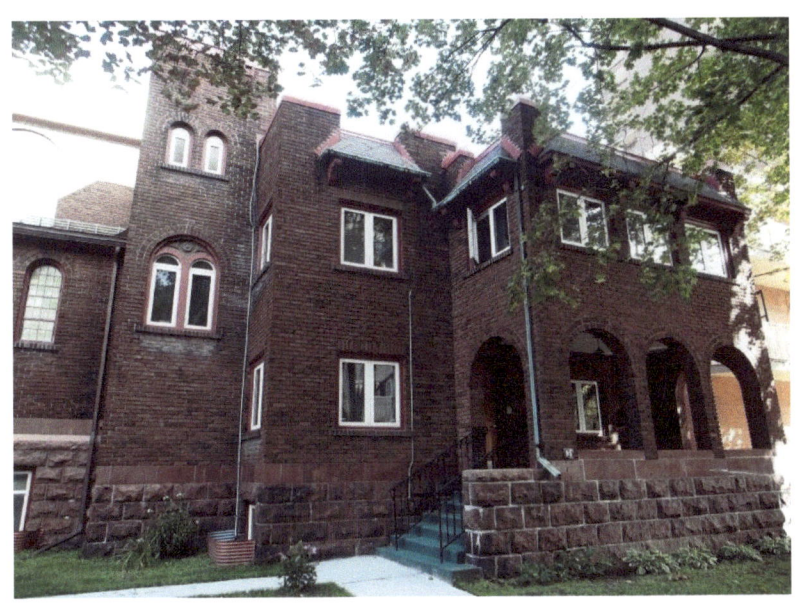

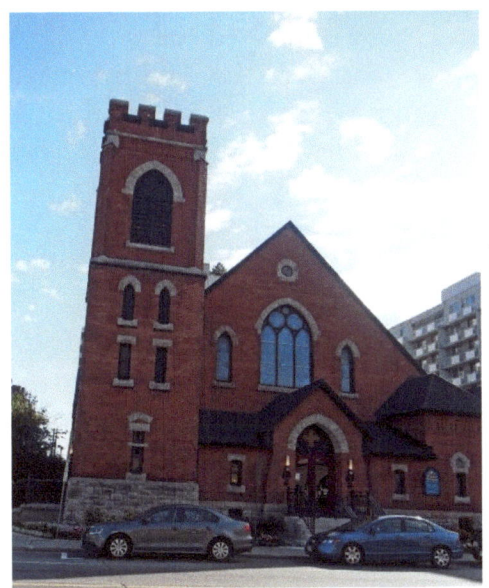

154 Somerset Street West (corner of Elgin) - St. John the
Evangelist Church – Gothic Revival – lancet windows,
quatrefoil above portal, stone lintels and bands, crenellated
tower

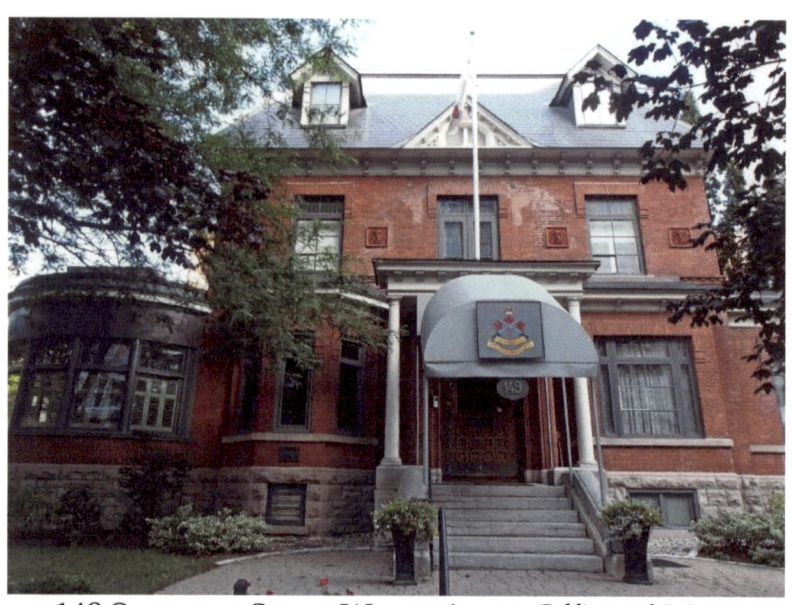

149 Somerset Street West - Army Officers' Mess
Pattee/Freiman House – 1891 – the home of two prominent
businessmen, Gordon B. Pattee, a lumberman, and later
Archibald K. Freiman, a merchant – Second Empire style,
mansard roof, dormers, terra cotta decorations

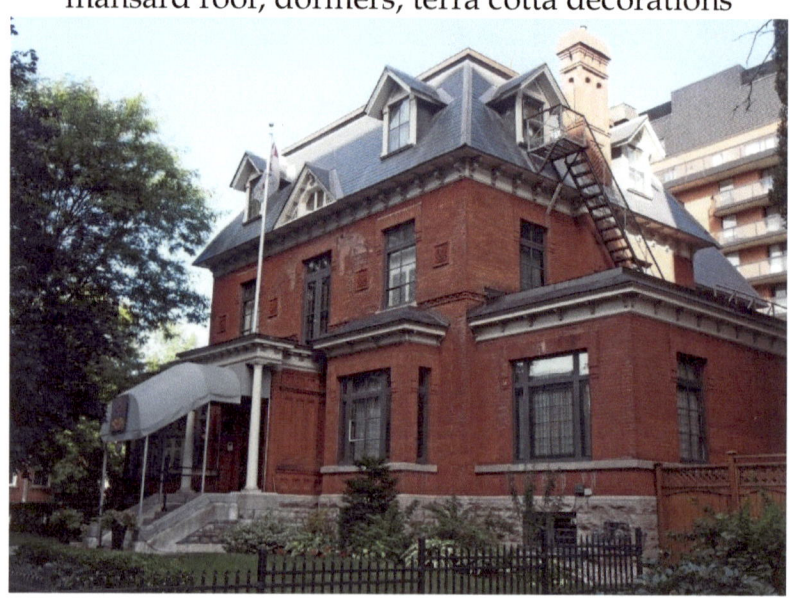

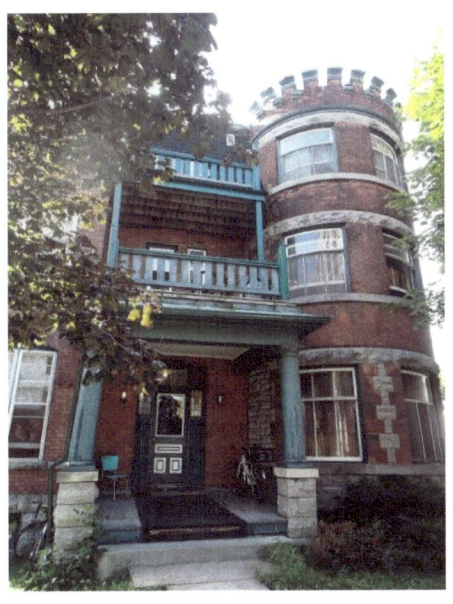

40 Cartier Street – crenelated tower, 2nd and 3rd floor balconies

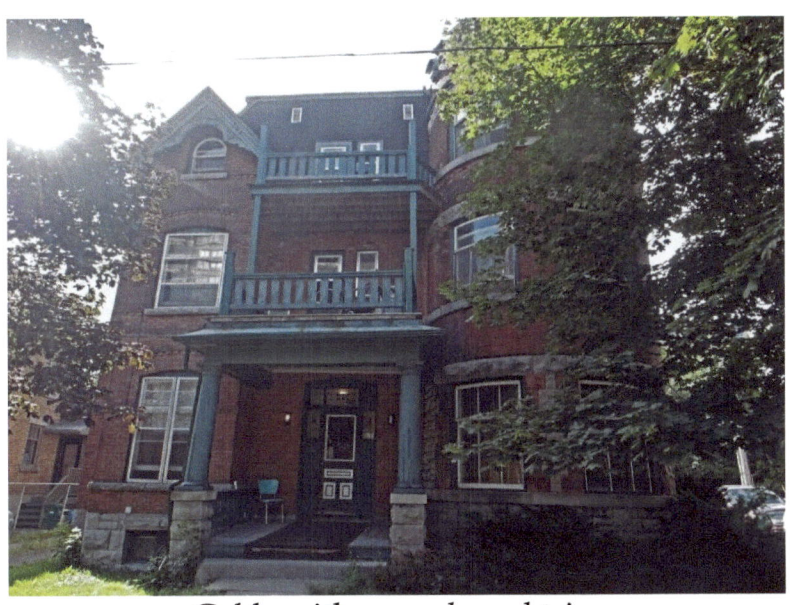

Gable with verge board trim

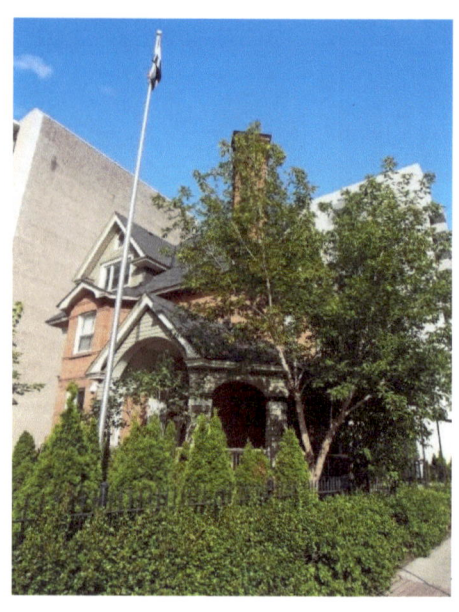

46 Cartier Street – 1901 - built for retired merchant Newell Bate – Queen Anne style with elaborate chimneys, porches and gables – Embassy of Syrian Arab Republic

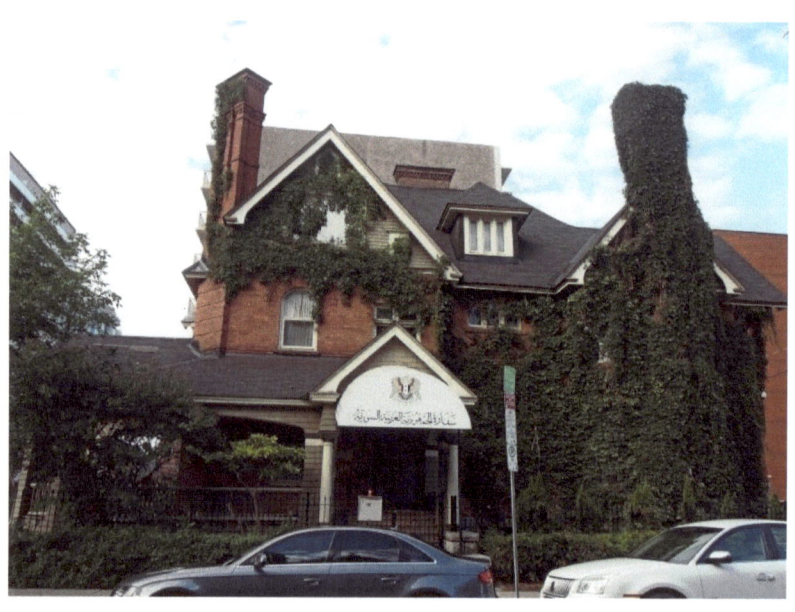

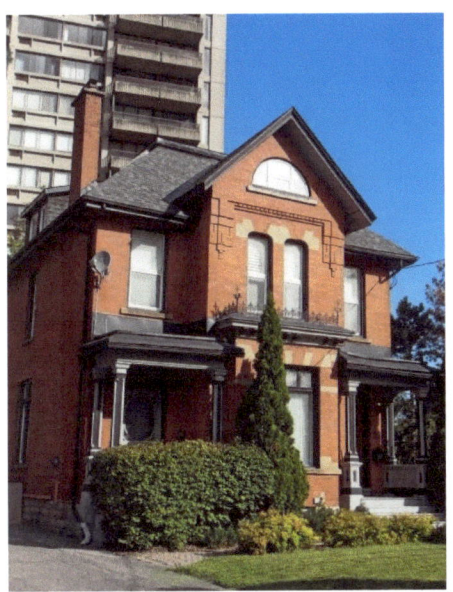

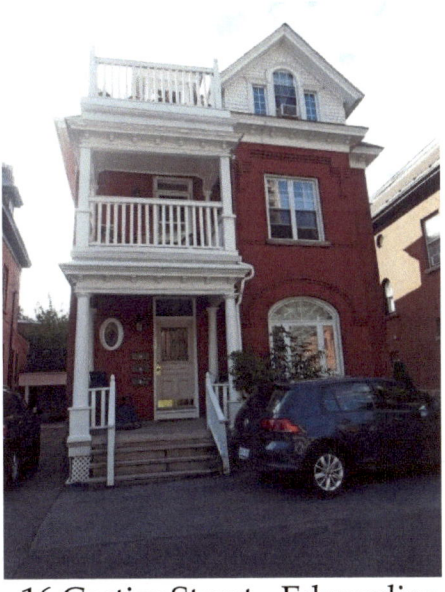

27 Cartier Street - frontispiece
Dichromatic brickwork

16 Cartier Street - Edwardian
Palladian window

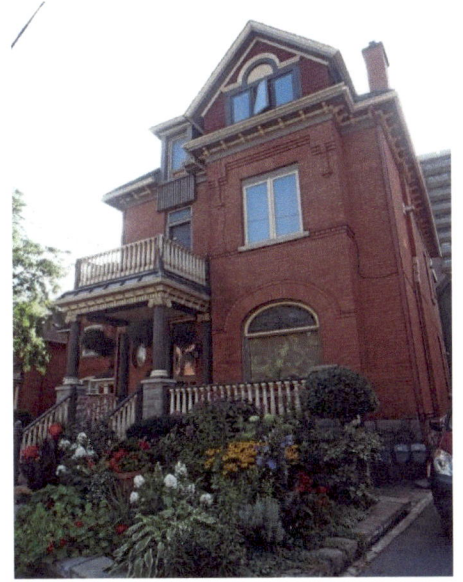

12 Cartier Street – Edwardian - voussoirs above stained glass
window, cornice brackets, Palladian window in gable, and
Ionic capitals on porch pillars with balcony above

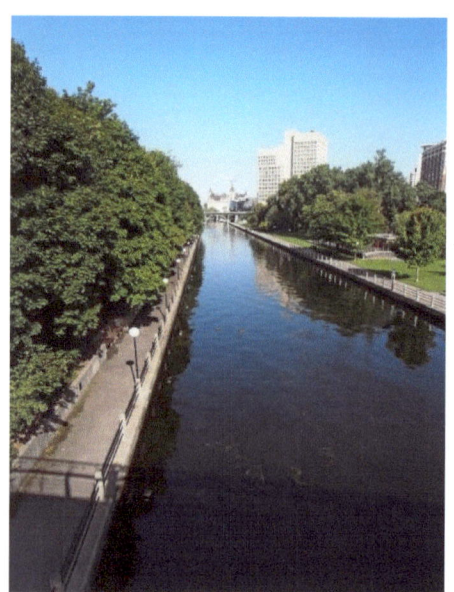
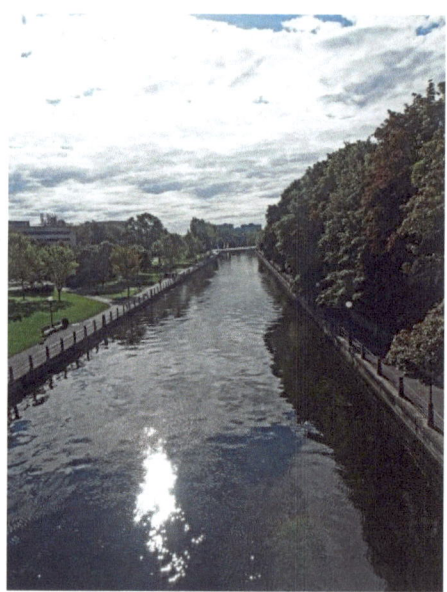

Rideau Canal

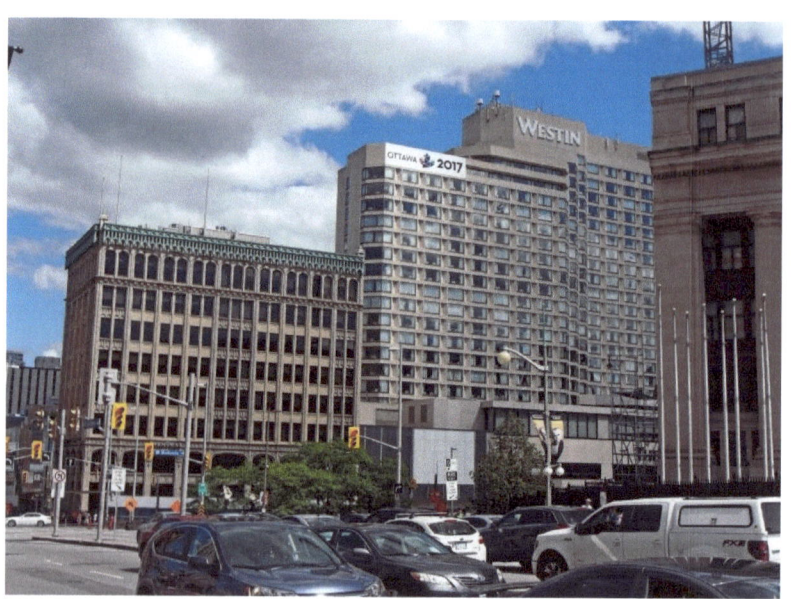

Mackenzie Avenue

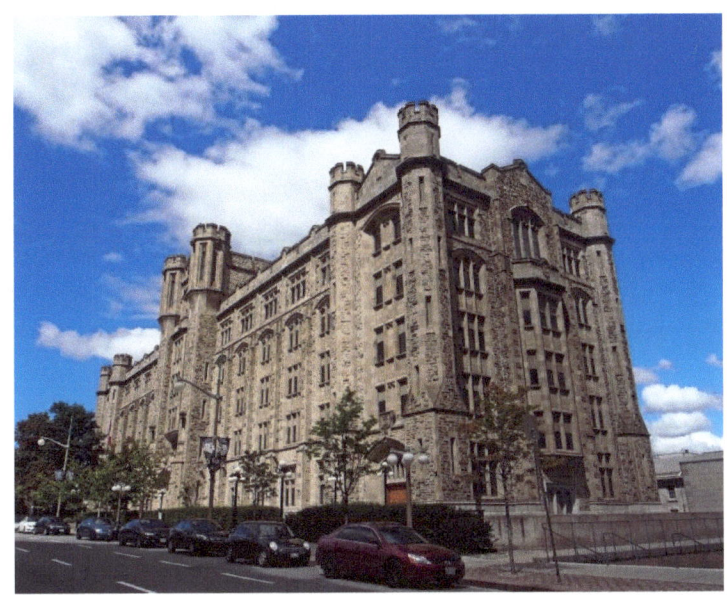

555 Mackenzie Avenue – The Connaught Building – 1913 – Tudor Gothic - named after the Duke of Connaught, third son of Queen Victoria, who served as 10th Governor General of Canada from 1911–16 – faced in rusticated sandstone, embellished with turrets, a crenellated roofline, buttresses, corbelling, niches, carved embellishments, an ogee arched entrance and rows of flat-headed windows accented by dressed quoins

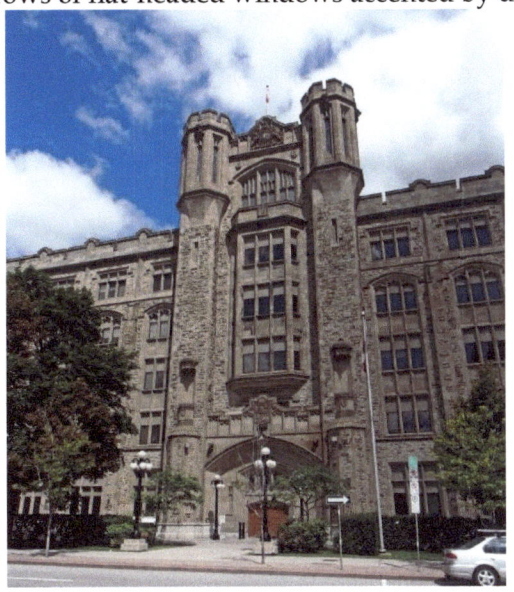

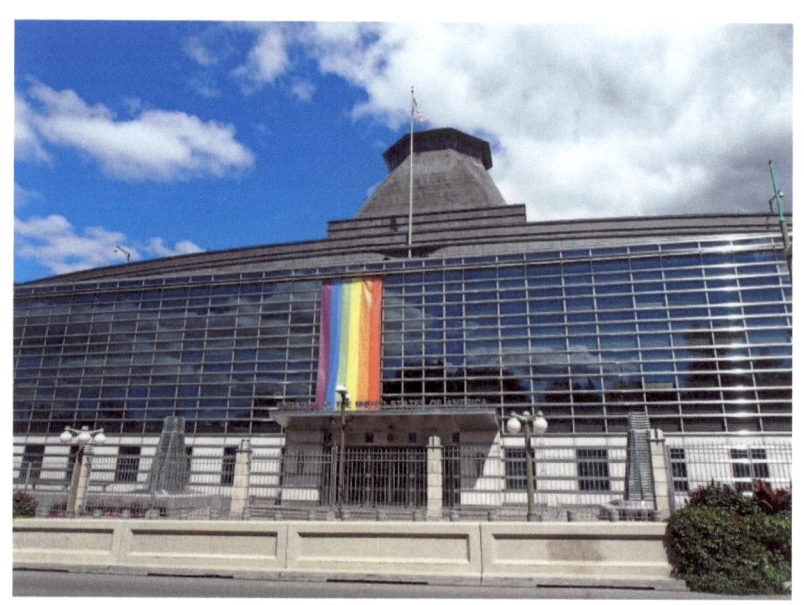

United States Embassy

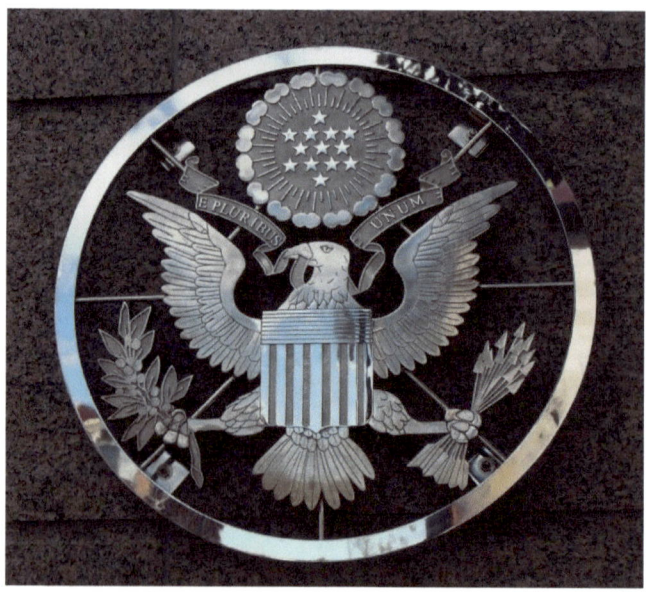

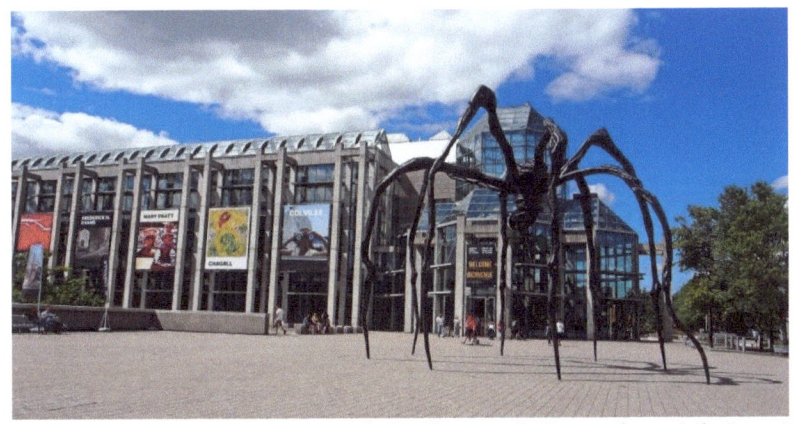

380 Sussex Drive - National Gallery of Canada with Louise Bourgeois' giant spider, *Maman* (1999) in front

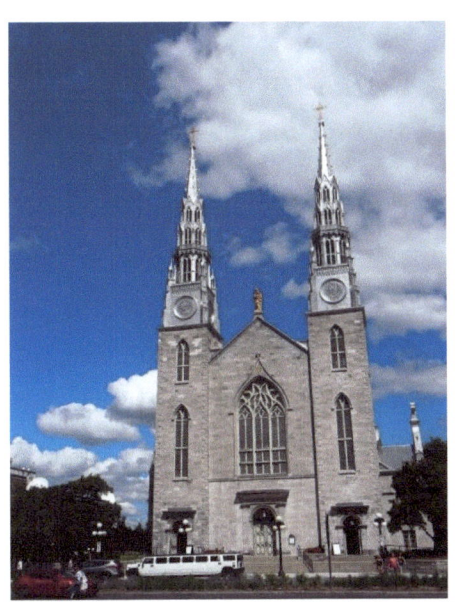

375 Sussex Drive - Notre-Dame Cathedral Basilica is a Roman Catholic Church – lower features (main entrance) are Neo-Classical, while the upper portions are Neo-Gothic – completed in 1846; the two Gothic spires added in 1866

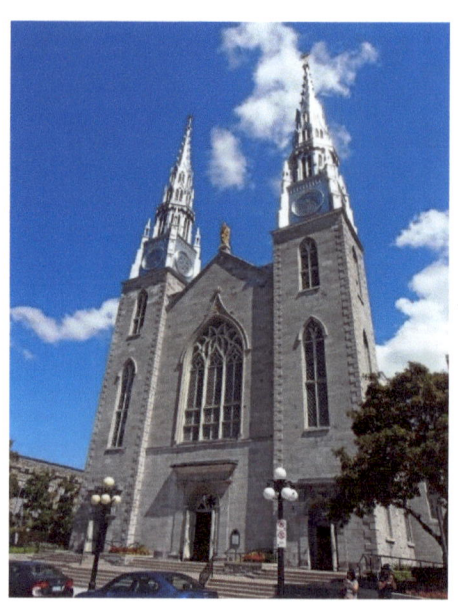

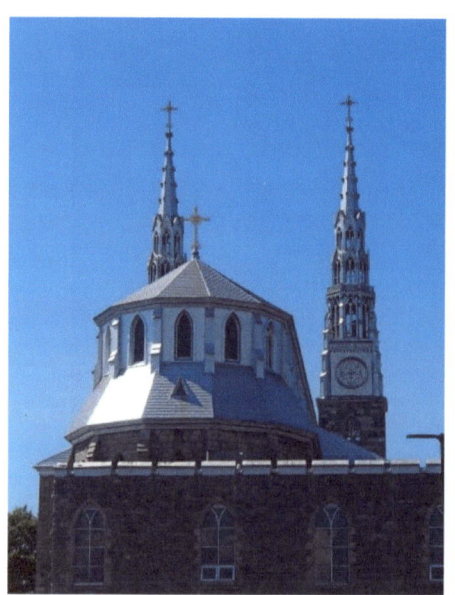
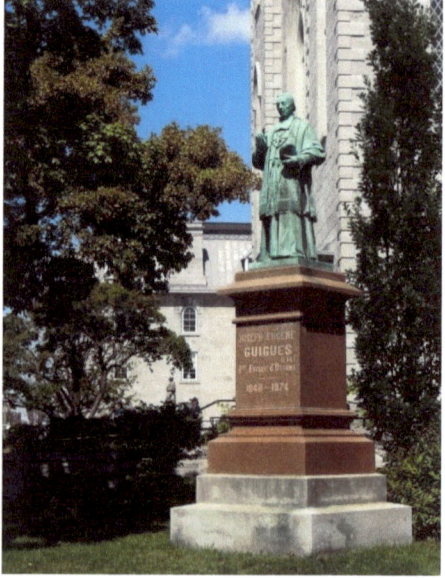

Joseph Eugene Guigues – 1848-1874 – a priest, a teacher and became the first bishop of the diocese of Bytown (Ottawa)

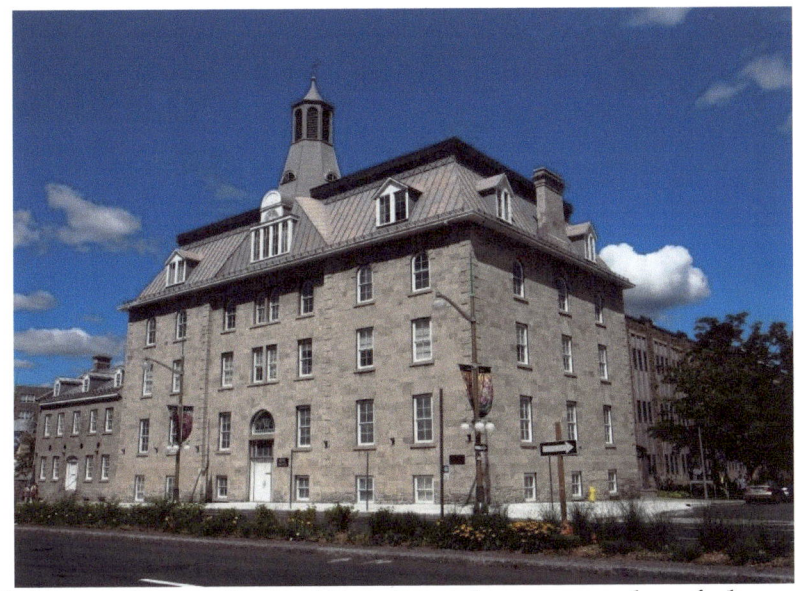

373 Sussex Drive – Second Empire style – mansard roof, dormers, cupola, corner quoins

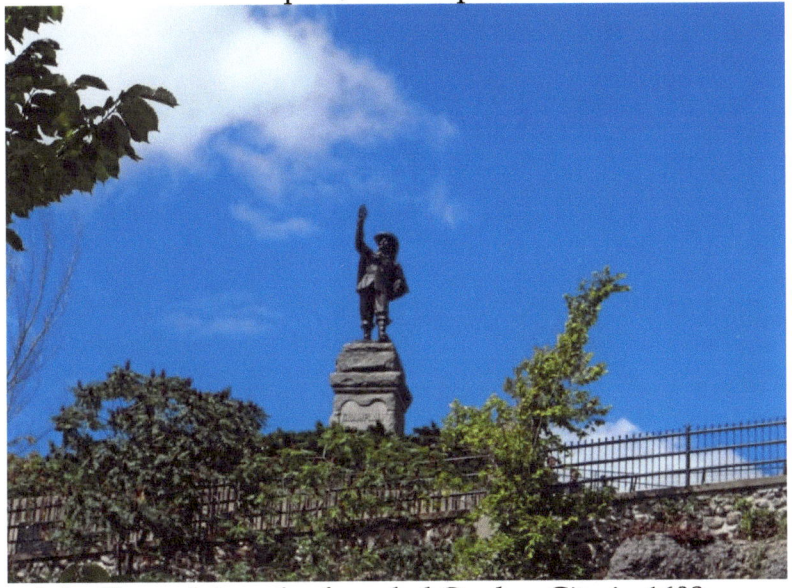

Samuel de Champlain, who founded Quebec City in 1608, was one of the first Europeans to explore Canada. He first traveled the Ottawa River in 1613, keeping a journal and taking measurements with an astrolabe (ordinarily used for navigation at sea).

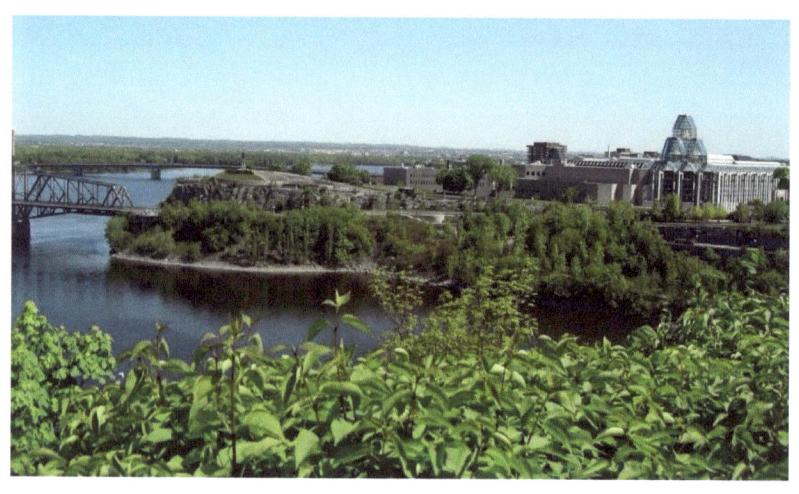

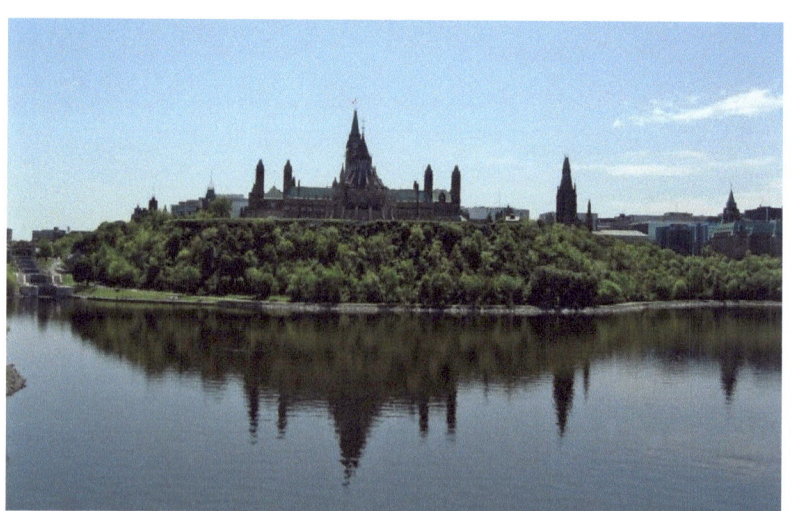

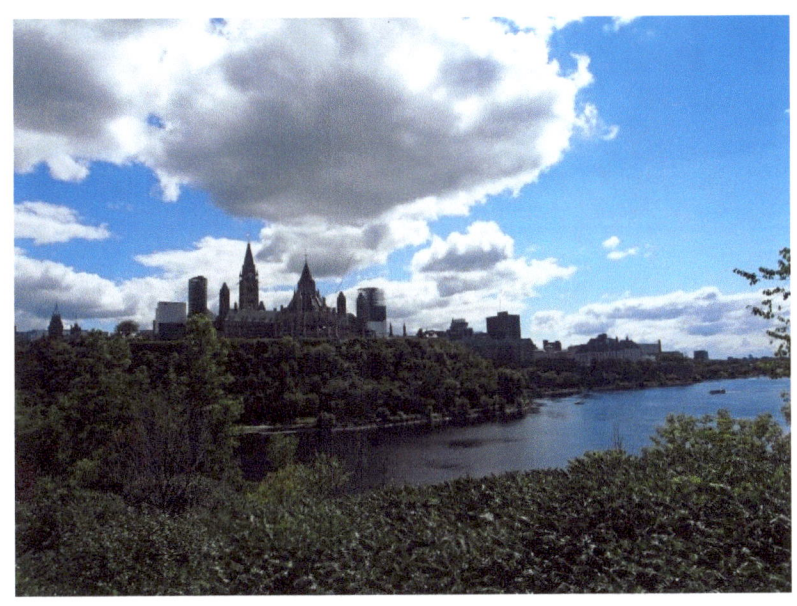

Ottawa River

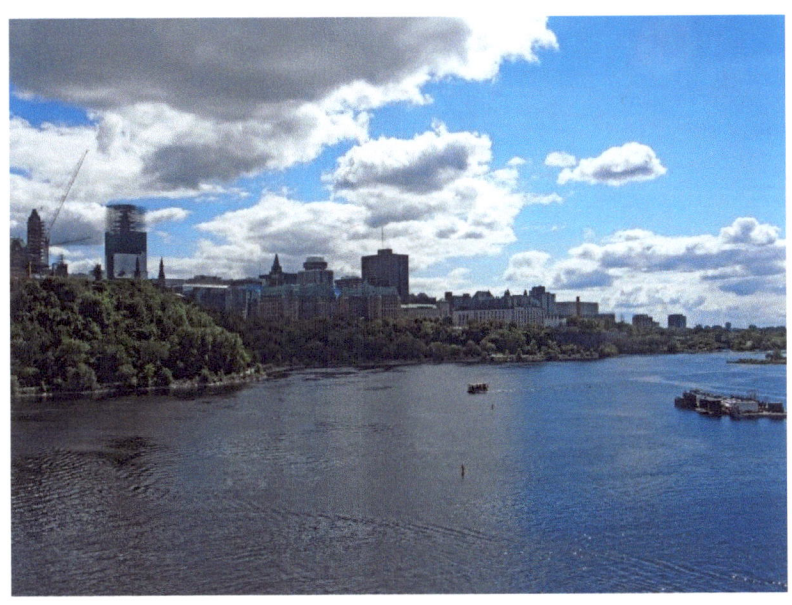

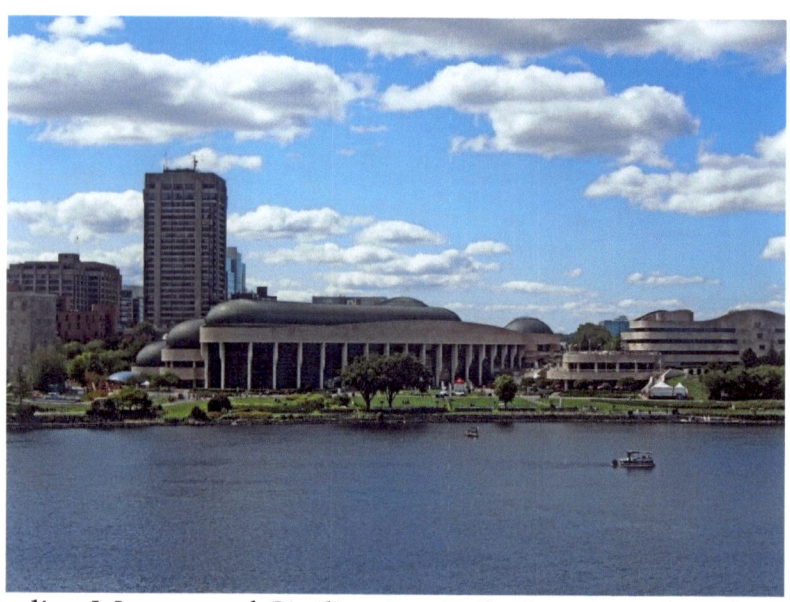

Canadian Museum of Civilization is the largest cultural attraction in Canada. It is located across the Ottawa River in Gatineau, Quebec. The museum buildings were designed by Native-Canadian architect Douglas Cardinal. It is famous for its curved lines, domed roofs, and monumental size. Its exterior is faced with limestone from Manitoba, and its roof is made of Canadian copper. One of the most popular attractions is the historic panorama known as the Canada Hall with 1000 years of Canadian history under one dome.

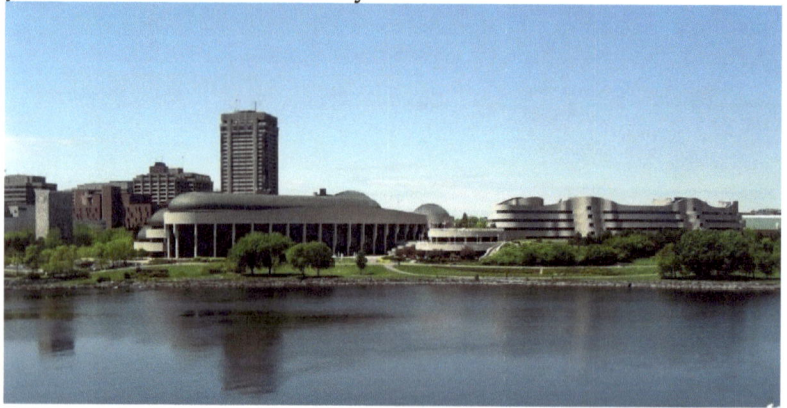

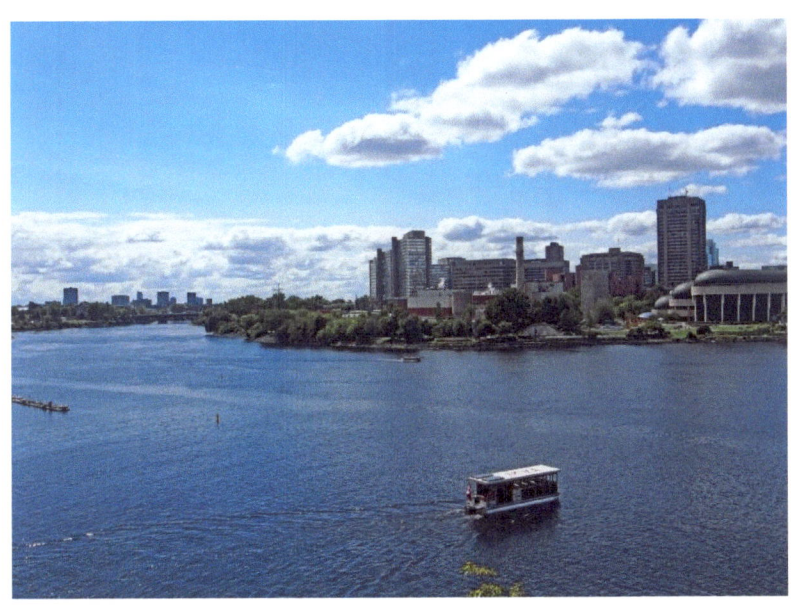

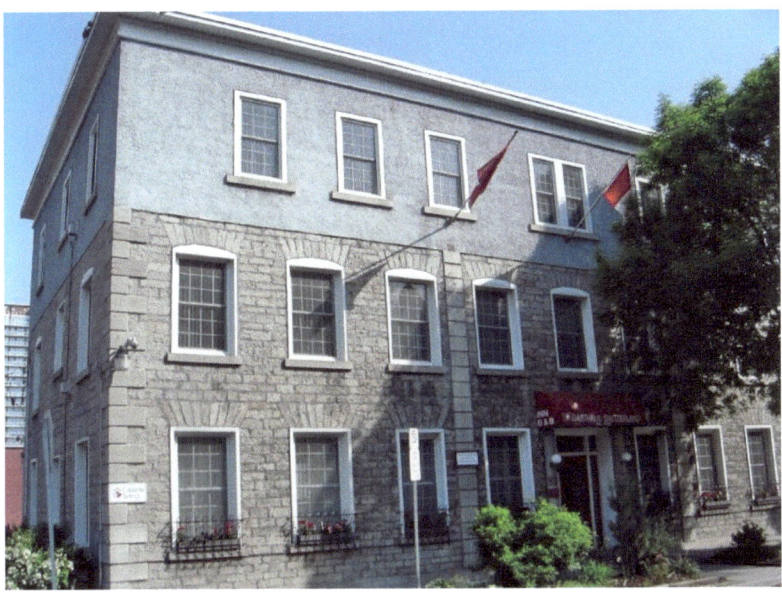

89 Daly Avenue - Gasthaus Switzerland Inn Bed and Breakfast
– now Swiss Hotel - located in the heart of downtown Ottawa
- a European-style hotel with a modern flair, reclaimed
hardwood floors

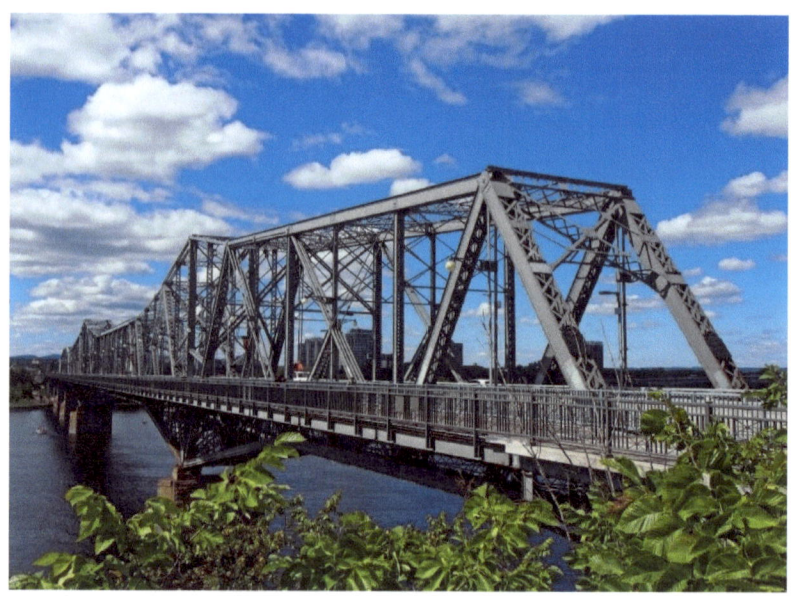

Alexandra Bridge – opened in 1901 – link between Ottawa and Gatineau (formerly Hull)

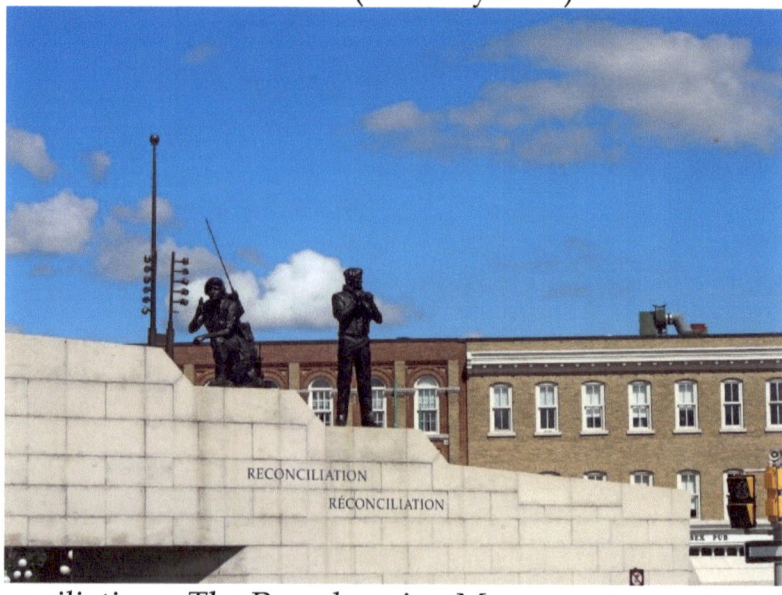

Reconciliation – The Peacekeeping Monument – contrasts the chaos of war with the order and safety of peace, and symbolizes the resolution of conflict

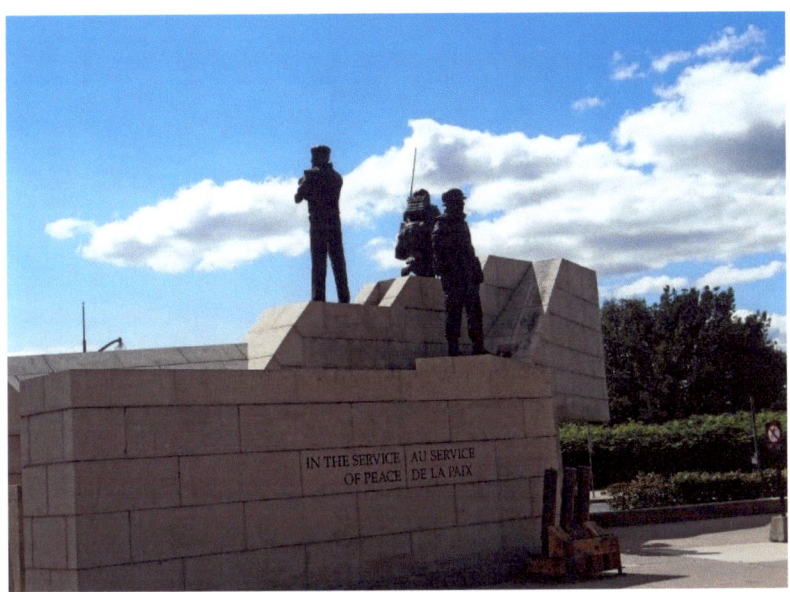

In the Service of Peace

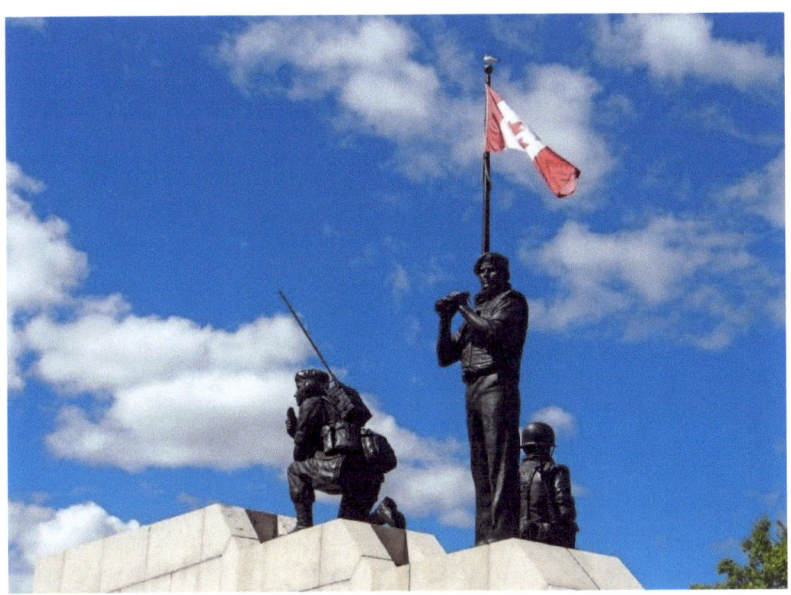

Tells the story of United Nations peacekeepers - Lester B. Pearson won the Nobel Peace Prize in 1957 for his success in establishing this international force

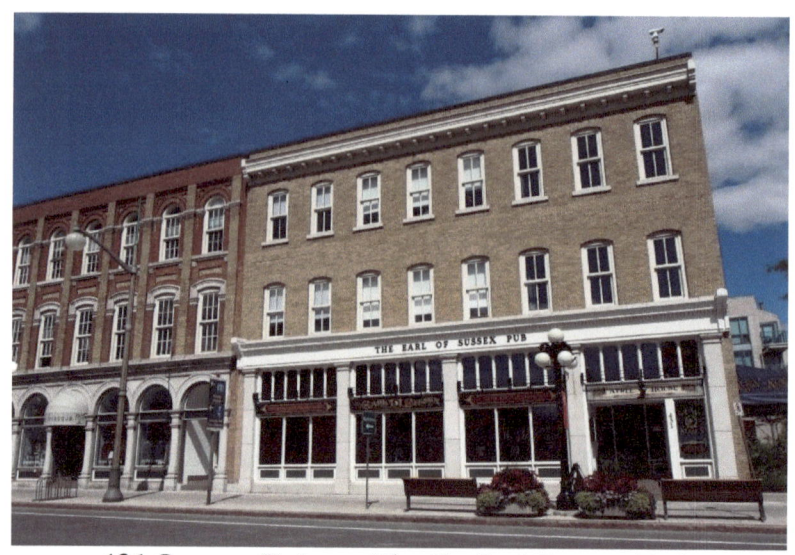

431 Sussex Drive - The Earl of Sussex Pub

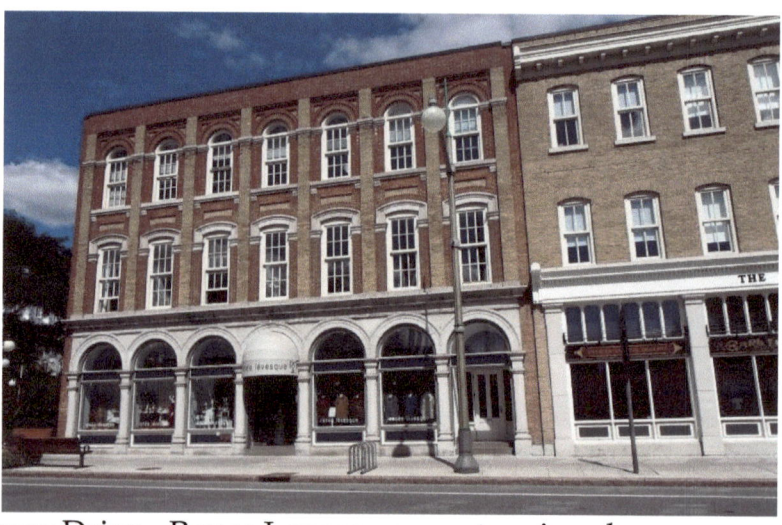

Sussex Drive - Renee Levesque - custom jewelry, accessories
and unique clothing – pilasters, voussoirs

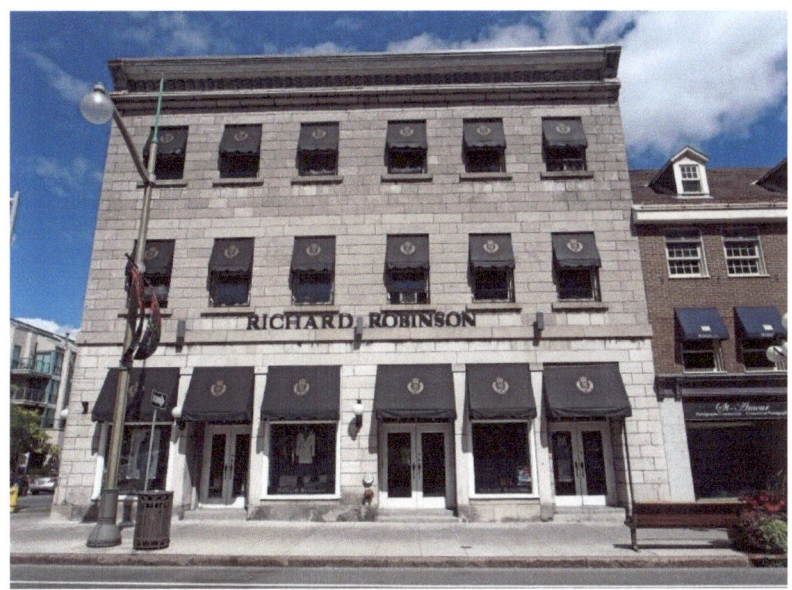

419 Sussex Drive - Richard Robinson Haute Couture selling designer fashions from the main floor and teaching designers in their Academy of Fashion Design on the top floors

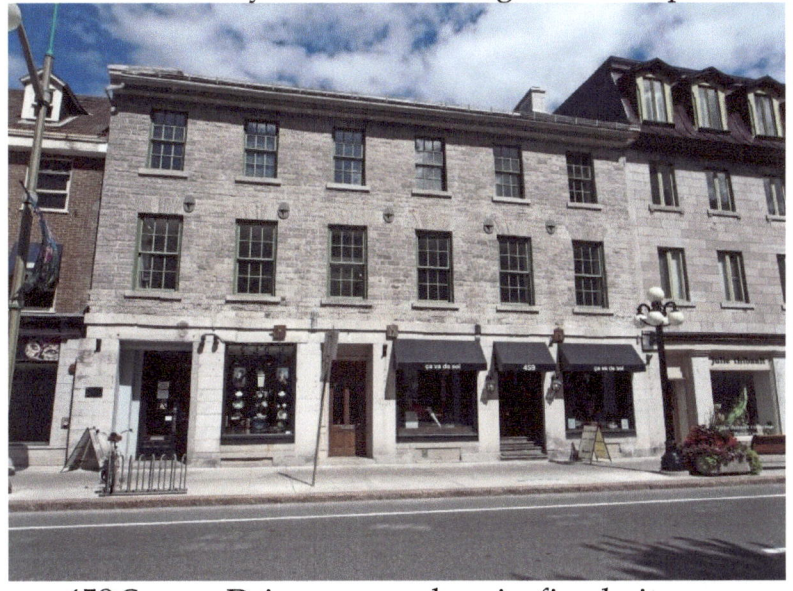

459 Sussex Drive – ca va de soi – fine knitwear – stone building

The restored shopfronts along one side of Sussex Drive are relics of businesses that once served the lumber trade in the Ottawa Valley where wood was king in the 19th century. Forest industries turned Ottawa into a booming mill town and the shops on this street into bustling centres of commerce.

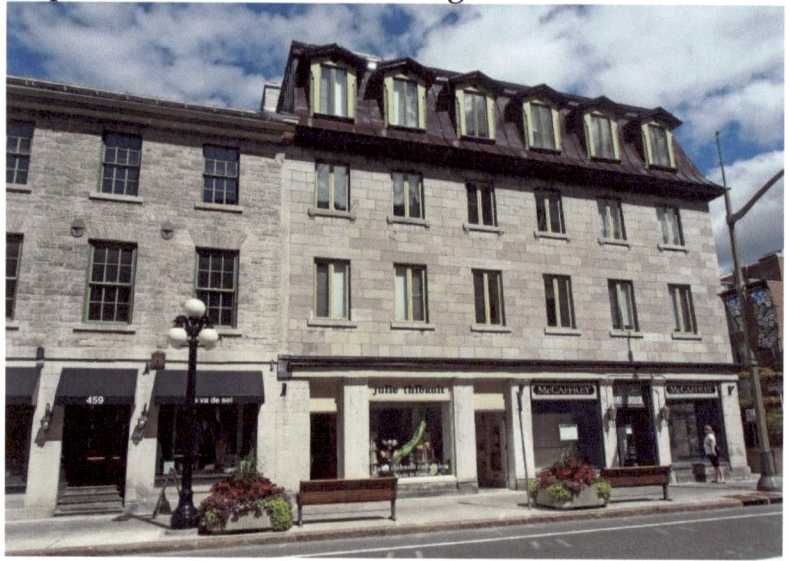

459-465 Sussex Drive - dormers

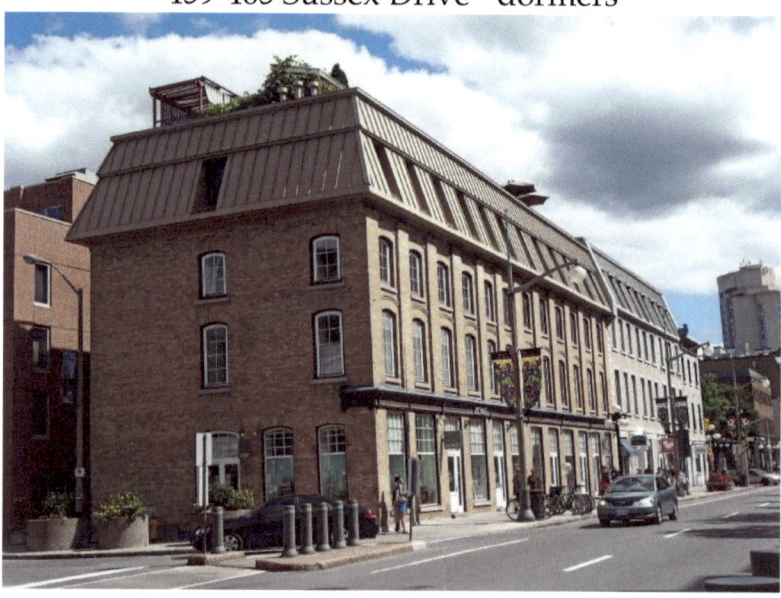

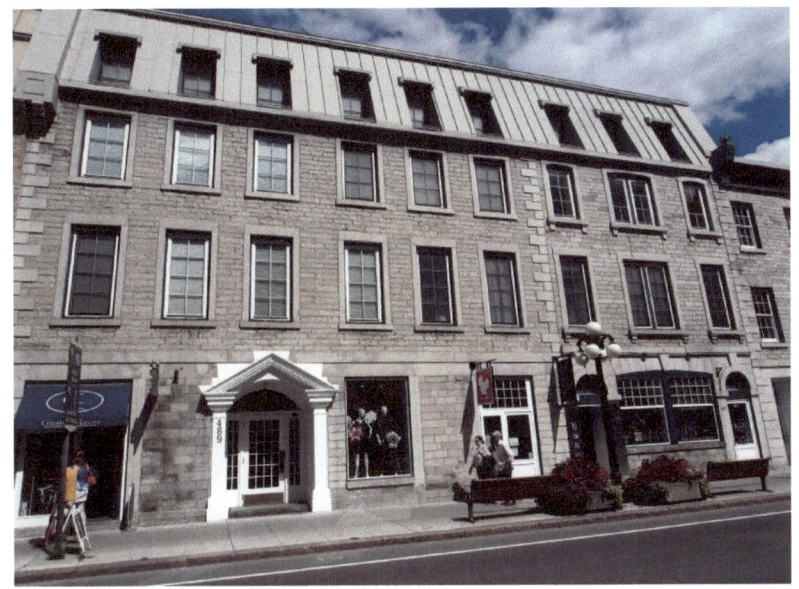

489 Sussex Drive – corner quoins, open pediment above door

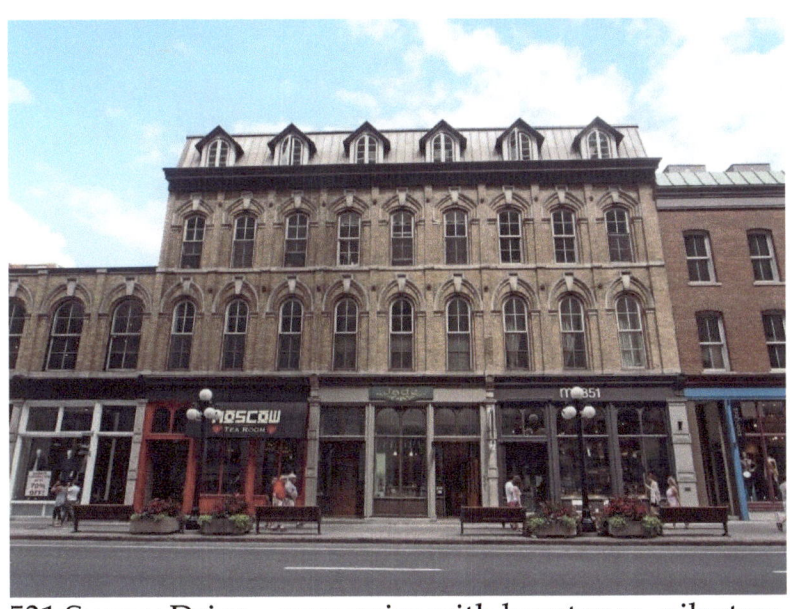

531 Sussex Drive – voussoirs with keystones, pilasters, dormers, bands dividing floors

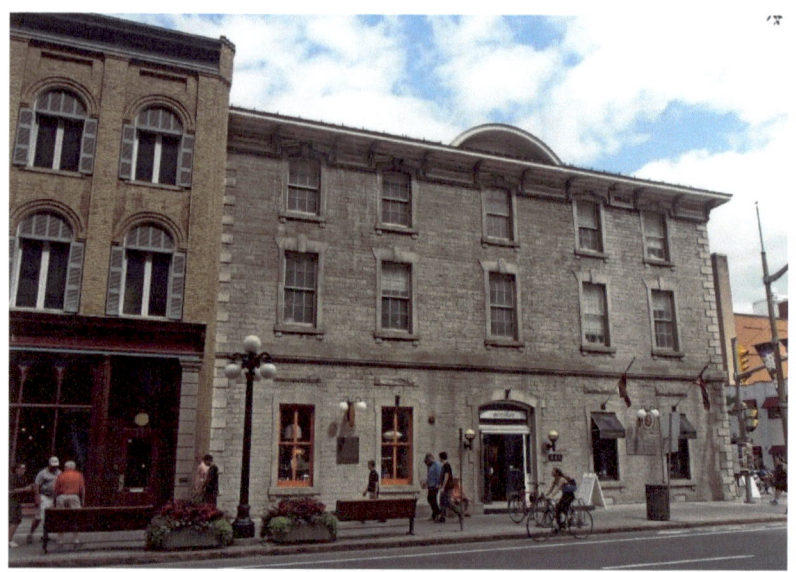

541 Sussex Drive – stone, corner quoins, keystones, cornice brackets

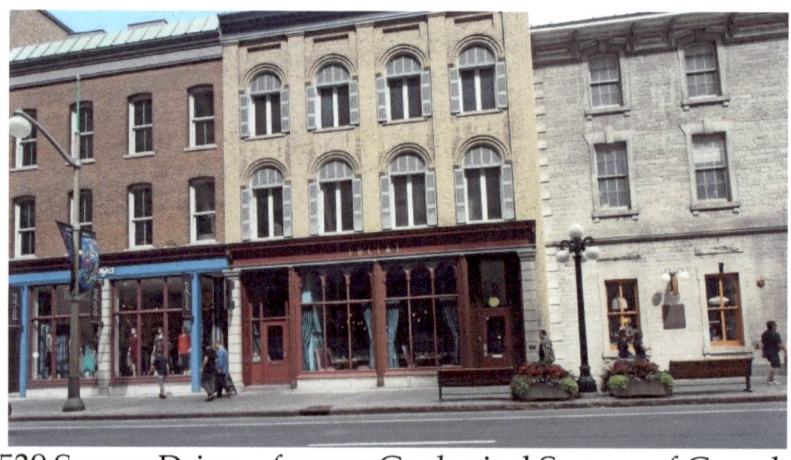

539 Sussex Drive – former Geological Survey of Canada building on right - mid-19th century hotel

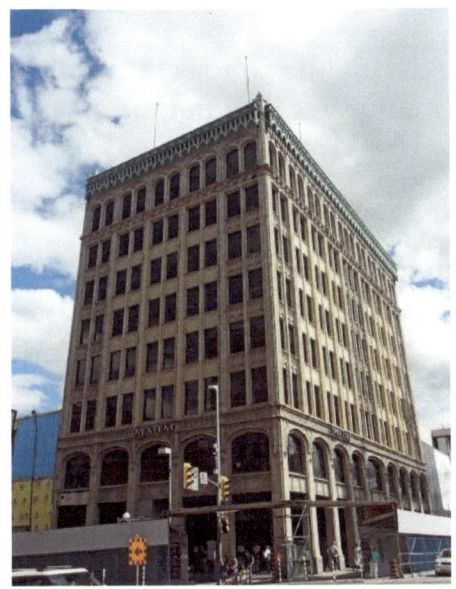

10 Rideau Street - Open Text – the leader in information management

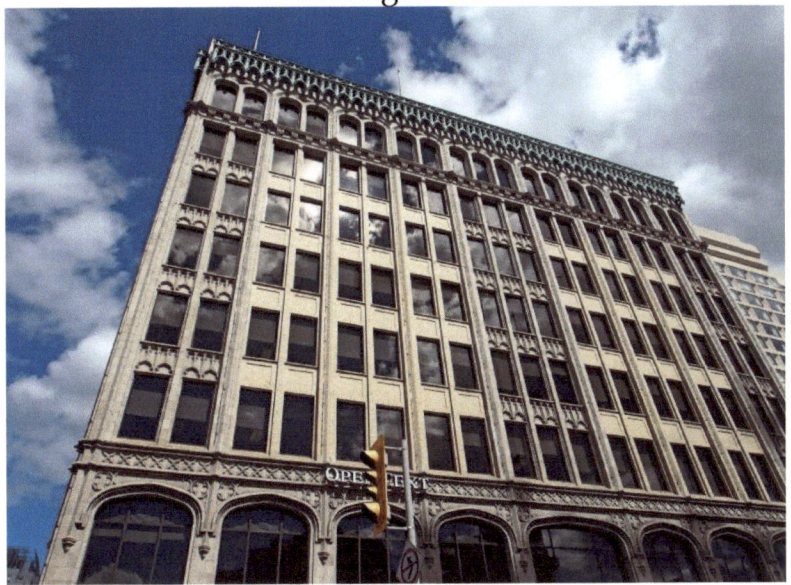

Decorative cornice, decorative band below top floor, other decorative panels, quatrefoil decorations on second floor above windows

Architectural Terms

Bay Window: A window that projects out from a wall, in a semicircular, rectangular, or polygonal design. Used frequently in Gothic and Victorian designs. Example: Elgin Street, Page 11	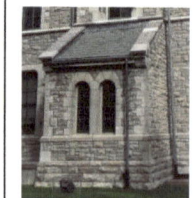
Brackets: a decorative or weight-bearing structural element which forms a right angle with one side against a wall and the other under a projecting surface such as an eave or roof. Example: 44-50 Sparks Street, Page 7	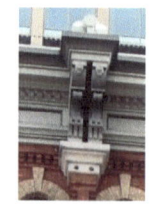
Buttress: a masonry structure built against or projecting from a wall which serves to support or reinforce the wall. In Canadian architecture, they are sometimes used for decoration. Example: 140 Laurier Avenue West, Page 12	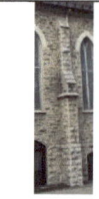
Capital: The uppermost finish or decoration on a column. A Corinthian column is characterized by a rounded capital decorated with acanthus leaves and a square abacus (the uppermost portion of a capital directly below the entablature) on tall slender columns. Example: 167 Sparks Street, Page 8 A Composite is a mixture of two or sometimes, three, of the major styles – Ionic, Doric, and Corinthian. Example: 280 Gilmour Street, Page 21	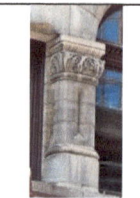 Corinthian 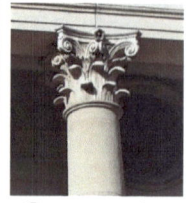 Composite

Corbel: Corbelling is the original method of making arches a series of stones or bricks that protrude beyond the lower level to finally cover the arch. Corbels are used to support cornices, turrets, brackets, ribs and oriel windows. A corbel is also a stone or piece of wood that supports a super incumbent weight. Example: 555 Mackenzie Avenue, Page 33	
Cornice: originally the wooden overhang of the roof. With the use of stone, brick, iron and steel, the cornice is any horizontal moulded projection at the top of a building. They can be very decorative. Example: old Ottawa Normal School, Page 10	
Crenellation: a series of depressed openings, like a battlement, but with more space between the openings. A crenelle (or kernel) in medieval times was an opening in a battlement, a loophole through which arrows and missiles could be launched. Example: 306 Metcalfe Street, Page 19	
Cupola: A domed or curved roof rising from a building as a decorative element. Example: 373 Sussex Drive, Page 37	
Dentil Moulding: an even series of rectangles used as ornamental decoration in cornices. Example: 167 Sparks Street, Page 8	

Dichromatic brickwork: the use of two colours of brick, tile or slate to decorate a façade. This is an example of multi-coloured masonry. Example: 44-50 Sparks Street, Page 7	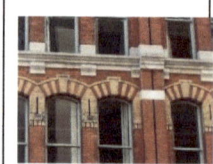
Dormer: (French for "sleep") a gable end window that pierces through the plane of a sloping roof surface to create usable space in the top floor or attic of a building by adding headroom. Example: 149 Somerset Street West, Page 28	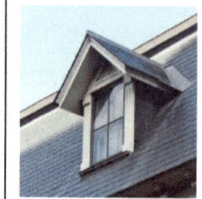
Foil: an architectural device based on a symmetrical rendering of leaf shapes, defined by overlapping circles that produce a series of cusps to make a lobe. The number of cusps can be three (trefoil), four (quatrefoil) or five (cinquefoil), or can be any number (multifoil). Trefoil Example: 152 Metcalfe Street, Page 14 Quatrefoil Example: 10 Rideau Street, Page 49	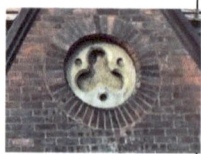 Trefoil 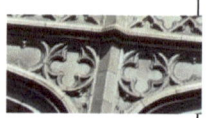 Quatrefoil
Fretwork: interlaced decorative design resembling a bracket Example: 301 Metcalfe Street, Page 18	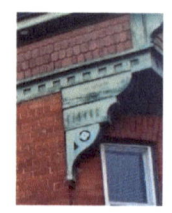

Frontispiece: a portion of the façade of a building, usually a centred doorway that is slightly raised from the rest of the building, usually has extensive ornamentation. Frontispieces are usually Classical in design with white columned porches. Example: Elgin Street, Page 10	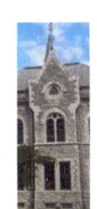
Gable: the triangular portion of a wall between the edges of a sloping roof. Example: 27 Cartier Street, Page 28 **Jacobean Gable:** the gable extends above the roofline. Example: Elgin Street, Page 10	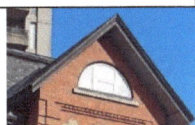 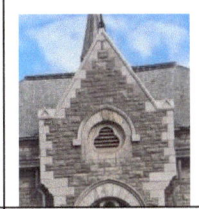
Iron Cresting: A decorative ornament along the top of a roof. Iron cresting was popular in the Baroque era and also in Italianate, Victorian, Second Empire and Queen Anne styles of architecture. Example: Elgin Street, Page 10	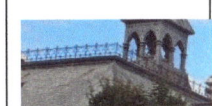
Keystones and Voussoirs: a voussoir is a wedge-shaped element used in building an arch. A keystone is the central stone that locks all the stones into position, allowing the arch to bear weight. A keystone is often enlarged and embellished. Example: 185-187 Sparks Street, Page 8	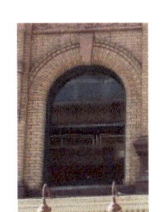
Lancet Window: a tall, narrow window with a pointed arch at its top. Example: 140 Laurier Avenue West, Page 12	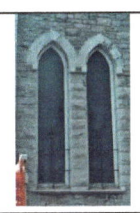

Lintel: horizontal part above a window or door that supports the structure above it. Example: 154 Somerset Street West, Page 27	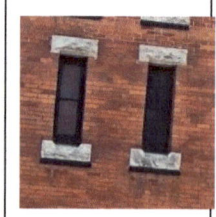
Mansard Roof: This style was popularized by Francois Mansart (1598-1666), an accomplished architect of the French Baroque period and especially fashionable during the Second French Empire (1852-1870). This roof is almost flat on the top section, with two slopes on each of its sides with the lower slope at a steeper angle than the upper and having dormer windows. Example: 149 Somerset Street West, Page 28	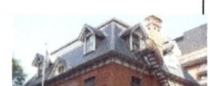
Oriel Window - These small areas were originally set into walls and galleries for the purpose of private prayer. Over time, any projecting window or area on an upper floor was called an oriel. Example: 100 Elgin Street, Page 22	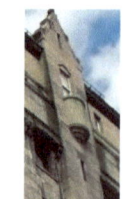
Palladian Window: a large window that is divided into three sections with the centre section larger than the two side sections and usually arched. Example: 16 Cartier Street, Page 31	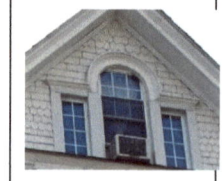
Pediment: a triangular section above the door or portico, usually supported by columns. The inside of the triangle is called the tympanum. Example: 280 Gilmour Street, Page 21	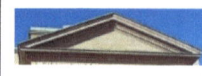

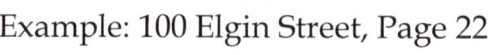
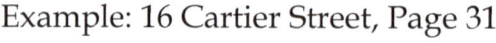

Pilaster: a slightly projecting column built into or applied to the face of a wall for additional structural support. Example: 185-187 Sparks Street, Page 9	
Portal: is an opening in a wall of a building, gate or fortification, especially a grand entrance to an important structure. Example: 152 Metcalfe Street, Page 14	
Quoin: masonry blocks at the corner of a wall, often a decorative feature, usually larger or of a different colour than the rest of the wall. Example: 489 Sussex Drive, Page 47	
Rose Window: a circular window with ornamental tracery radiating from the centre. Example: 152 Metcalfe Street, Page 14	
Scalloping: In Gothic or Medieval architecture, scalloping was used as decoration under a cornice or decorative frieze. The design may come from the machicolations in turrets. The brackets used to support the openings for attack gradually became more decorative. Example: Page 10	

Turret: a small tower that projects from the wall of a building. Example: 555 Mackenzie Avenue, Page 33	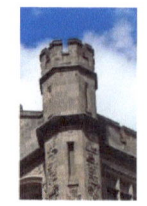
Verge board and Finial: also called bargeboards – hang from the projecting end of a roof and are often elaborately carved and ornamented. **Finial:** ornament added to the top of a gable, pinnacle, canopy or spire – a Gothic element. Example: 296 Metcalfe Street, Page 18	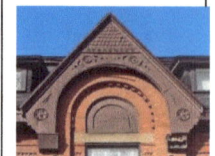
Wimperg: A wimperg is a German and Dutch word for an ornamental gable with tracery (stonework elements that support the glass in a window) over windows or portals, which were often accompanied with pinnacles. It was a typical element in Gothic Architecture, especially in cathedral architecture. Wimpergs often had crockets or other decorative elements. The intention behind the wimperg was the perception of increased height. Example: 120 Lisgar Street, Page 13	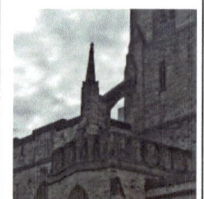
Window Hood: A **hood** is the piece found above window openings, usually of an ornate design, and covers the top third of the opening. Hoods are commonly placed above arched or curved openings on both windows and doors. Example: 236 Metcalfe Street, Page 15	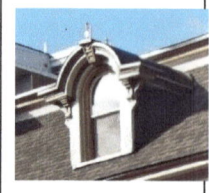

Building Styles

Art Deco, 1910-1940 - The Art Deco Style was developed for the French luxury market after World War I. Art Deco left its mark on everything from lamps and foot stools to purses and hair combs. The style was adopted in Ontario by wealthy and very fashionable patrons who wanted Art Deco detailing to make their buildings look lavish and exotic. Example: 144 Wellington Street, Page 10	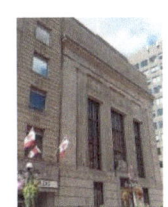
Baronial Gothic is a style of architecture that draws on the features of Medieval castles, tower houses and the French Renaissance châteaux. Buildings of the style frequently feature towers adorned by small turrets, roof lines are uneven, their crenelated battlements often broken by stepped gables. While small lancet windows may appear in towers and gables, large bay windows of plate glass were not uncommon, but even these often had their individual roofs adorned by pinnacles and crenelation. Porches, porticos and porte-cocheres were often given the castle treatment. An imitation portcullis on the larger houses was sometimes suspended above a front door, flanked by heraldic beasts and other medieval architectural motifs. Example: 306 Metcalfe Street, Page 19	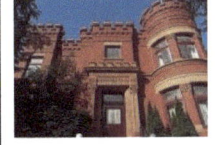

Château (1880 - 1930): The Château Style is a grand adaptation of the sixteenth-century French chateaux of the Loire Valley. The fortified castles of medieval France were translated in Ontario into asymmetrical, irregular and equally elegant hotels, convents, and imposing private houses for the wealthy. The bases of this style are steeply pitched roofs with plenty of dormers, turrets, gables, conical towers, lunettes, and iron cresting. Ornamentation is lavish with intricate string courses, corbel tables, finials and crockets. The walls are generally finished stone or stucco and the roofs are often copper left to develop a patina of soft green. Château style can be distinguished from Italian Villa and Queen Anne Revival by the roof line and pitch. Example: 59 Sparks Street, Page 6	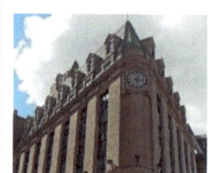
Edwardian, 1900-1930 – This style bridges the ornate and elaborate styles of the Victorian era and the simplified styles of the 20th century. Balanced facades, simple roof lines, dormer windows, large front porches, and smooth brick surfaces are its characteristics. Example: 16 Cartier Street, Page 31	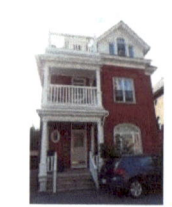
Gothic Revival, 1830-1890 – These decorative buildings have sharply-pitched gables with highly detailed verge boards, pointed-arch window openings, and dichromatic brickwork. It is a common style in Ontario. Example: 120 Lisgar Street, Page 13	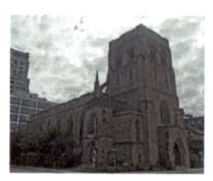

Italianate, 1850-1900 – A two story rectangular building with a mild hip roof, a projecting frontispiece, and generous eaves with ornate cornice brackets was the basis of the style; often there are large sash windows, quoins, ornate detailing on the windows, belvederes and wraparound verandahs. Italianate commercial buildings often have cast iron cresting and elegant window surrounds. Example: 44-50 Sparks Street, Page 7	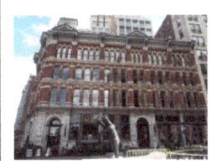
Neo-Classical (1810 - 1850) – This style was a direct result of the War of 1812. Many Upper Canadians returning from the war with the United States were second or third generation Loyalists who had inherited land and means from their forefathers. Once the conflict had passed, they had the money and the time to expand their holdings and indulge their architectural whims. Both residential and commercial buildings were constructed on the traditional Georgian plan, but they had a new gaiety and light-heartedness. Detailing became more refined, delicate, and elegant. Example: 375 Sussex Drive, Page 35	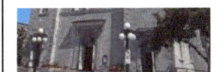

Neo-Gothic (Collegiate Gothic): is monochromatic and on a much grander scale than Gothic. Early neo-Gothic churches were often plastered or painted, later neo-Gothic churches were not. An important moment in the development of neo-Gothic is the year 1853, when the hierarchy of the Roman Catholic church was fully restored in the Netherlands. Materials used were natural stone combined with brick. Around the year 1850 neo-Gothicism was maturing and increasingly became a Roman Catholic style almost exclusively. Wall buttresses and finials are added, but they are generally far too small to be of any structural benefit. Example: 375 Sussex Drive, Page 35	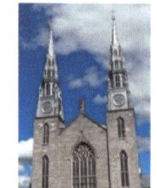
Queen Anne, 1885-1900 – This style is distinguished by an irregular outline featuring a combination of an offset tower, broad gables, projecting two-storey bays, verandahs, multi-sloped roofs, and tall, decorative chimneys. A mixture of brick and wood is common. Windows often have one large single-paned bottom sash and small panes in the upper sash. Example: 252 Metcalfe Street, Page 17	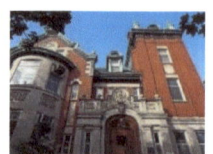
Romanesque Revival, 1880-1910 – This style hearkens back to medieval architecture of the 11th and 12th centuries with a heavy appearance, blocky towers and rounded arches. Example: 95 Somerset Street, Page 25	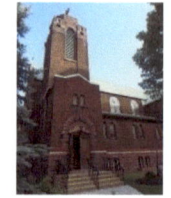

Tudor Revival – exposed timbers with stucco infill, multi-paned windows. Example: 555 Mackenzie Avenue, Page 33	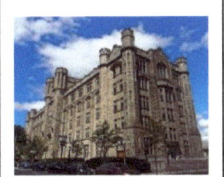
Vernacular/Traditional Mode 1638 - 1950 Influenced but not defined by a particular style, vernacular buildings are made from easily available materials and exhibit local design characteristics. Example: Somerset Street West, Page 24	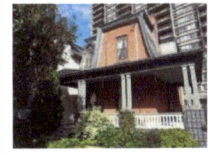
Victorian - In Ontario, a Victorian style building can be seen as any building built between 1840 and 1900 that doesn't fit into any of the other categories. It encompasses a large group of buildings constructed in brick, stone, and timber, using an eclectic mixture of Classical and Gothic motifs. Example: 296 Metcalfe Street, Page 18	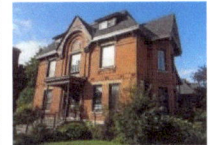

www.ingramcontent.com/pod-product-compliance
Lightning Source LLC
Chambersburg PA
CBHW040850180526
45159CB00001B/373